Picture credits

p12	TRIP/H. Rogers
p14	Ann and Bury Peerless
p23	Circa
p32	Still Pictures/Hartmut Schwarzbach
p33	Circa/Bipin J. Mistry
p40	Robert Harding/Mohamed Amin
p47	Tony Stone Images/Bill Aron
p48	Circa/Barrie Searle
p55	TRIP/H. Rogers
p57	Circa/John Smith
p59	PA News
p60	Sonia Halliday/Jane Taylor
p62	TRIP/H. Rogers
p64	Down's Syndrome Association/Zac Macauley
p66	Popperfoto (top and middle); Camera Press (bottom)
p70	Still Pictures/Mark Edwards
p74	Magnum/Gideon Mendel
p77	Science Photo Library/US National Archives
p78	Pictor
p79	Tony Stone Images/Ken Fisher
p85	Camera Press/Richard Ellis
p86	Science Photo Library/CC Studio
p88	Still Pictures/David Drain
p89	Science Photo Library/European Space Agency

Published by BBC Educational Publishing,
BBC White City, 201 Wood Lane, London W12 7TS
First published 2000
© Libby Ahluwalia/Jon Mayled/BBC Worldwide
(Educational Publishing), 2000

ISBN: 0 563 46410 0

Printed in Great Britain by Bell & Bain Ltd., Glasgow

Religious Education

Libby Ahluwalia
(Senior Examiner, GCSE Religious Education and Religious Studies)

Jon Mayled
(Chief Examiner, GCSE Religious Education and Religious Studies)

Contents

Introduction

About BITESIZE Religious Education

BITESIZE Religious Education is a revision guide that has been specially put together to help you with your GCSE exams. You can tape the television programmes and watch them on video, work your way through the activities and suggestions in this book and access the Internet online service.

It's called BITESIZE Religious Education because it's been divided into manageable, bitesize pieces of revision – much better than doing hours of revision the day before your exam! The video programmes, which give you information and advice, can be watched as often as you want until you have grasped all the points. Many sections of the video tie in with units in the book, which is divided into small sections that you can work through one by one. If you still don't understand something, you can contact the online team who are there to help you.

How to use this book

KEY TO SYMBOLS

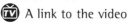 A link to the video

 A question to answer

 Useful advice

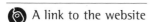 A link to the website

This book is divided into thirteen sections which cover the key GCSE topics of world religions and ultimate questions/moral and social issues. It especially focuses on the needs of students working on the short course syllabus. If you have any doubts about which topics you need to cover, ask your teacher.

Each unit of the book follows the same pattern:

- an introduction page which lists all the main areas for each topic

- Factzone pages, which give more detailed information about the beliefs of different people

- exam-type questions on each unit, with tips to help you understand what the examiners are looking for.

For many of the units, there are corresponding sections on the video. The video gives you extra information and tips on how to answer exam questions. It's a good idea to have the book open at the right Factzone page while you watch the video; then you can pause the programme and check your information as you revise. It's best to read the Factzone and watch the video before you try to answer the practice questions. It's also a good idea to write the time codes from the video on the relevant pages of the book – this will help you to find the right place on the video the next time you revise.

Most of the topics in Religious Education and Religious Studies courses from the different exam boards are covered in the book, except for papers which are about the study of the Bible – for example, Luke's Gospel. BITESIZE Religious Education does not aim to tell you everything you need to know about all the topics – you need to carry on using your school text books and the work you have done in class. But the practice questions, tips and suggestions will be useful for you, even if some of your topics do not appear in this book, because you will be practising the skills you need when answering questions on any topic.

Taken together, the book, video and website cover all the main skills required in GCSE Religious Education.

How to revise for GCSE Religious Education

There are three main aspects to successful revision; you will waste less time and achieve better results if you bear in mind the following:

- **organise**: prepare a long-term plan in order to make the most of your time
- **learn**: make sure you know the relevant facts
- **apply**: understand and practise how to answer different types of questions.

Organise

You need to draw up a revision timetable to cover all your subjects – not just Religious Education! It should begin three or four months (not days!) before your exams start. Your school may produce one which you could use, or you could adapt one to suit your own needs. Once you've drawn up an outline timetable, divide the days (say, 90 or 100) by the number of subjects you are taking. This will tell you how many days you've got for revising Religious Education. Three very important things about revision are:

1 Don't revise for more than about forty minutes at a time without a break as you will get too tired to learn properly. About three forty-minute sessions per night is enough for most people. Make sure you take breaks of at least ten or fifteen minutes between each session.

2 Be realistic – plan to have some time off, as well as time for revision. One complete day off and one night off a week is reasonable if you have started your revision early enough. Your work will be easier to remember if you come back to it from a break, and you need some time to relax with your friends. Don't forget to eat properly and get some fresh air and exercise every day!

3 Try to stick to your plan. If you cannot do the revision planned for a particular day because of illness or some other reason, re-organise your timetable to take account of this. If you start your revision early enough, there should be enough time to allow for unexpected illness, guests or other interruptions. However, be careful that you don't spend more time making new revision plans than you do on the revising itself!

Learn

Make sure that you know what the exam requirements are, such as the topics you should have covered, the ways in which questions are usually asked and the number of questions you have to answer in the exam. If in doubt, ask your teacher.

THE ON-LINE SERVICE
You can find extra support, tips and answers to your exam queries on the BITESIZE internet site. The address is http://www.bbc.co.uk/revision

Instead of copying out your notes or just reading your textbook, try some other ways of revising:

- highlight or underline key terms and facts in your notes
- write these key points on index cards, perhaps using brightly-coloured pens
- read out the main points into a tape recorder, and then play it back
- ask someone to test you on a topic
- make spider diagrams (see below) of the main points and key facts about topics on large pieces of paper. You could use colours and drawings, too.

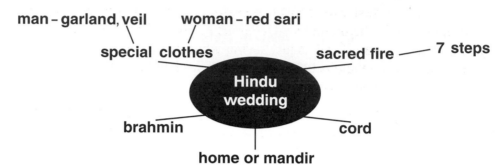

Then put the diagrams up on the wall in your bedroom or somewhere else where they will catch your eye.

- to learn new vocabulary, make two sets of cards in different colours – for example, use one piece of A4 card in blue and another in red. Cut the pieces of A4 into smaller cards. Write the new words on the blue cards and their meanings on the red cards. Shuffle the cards and then try to match each blue word card with its red partner. You could do this with a friend and see who can make the most pairs in the shortest time. Or you could take turns to test each other, reading out the meanings on the red cards and getting the other person to give you the right word.

- with a friend, talk about the 'evaluation' questions where you are asked to explain your opinion. Work out together how a believer might answer this question. Make sure you give your reasons every time you give an opinion.

Whatever methods you use for revision, try to find a warm, quiet place away from distractions. You will probably find that using several different methods of revising a topic is more interesting than using the same method over and over again.

Apply

Practising written answers to exam-type questions is just as important as learning the facts. For a revision session, you could read through the Factzone on a topic, watch the video sequence (if there is one) and then work through an example question. In particular, make sure you look at and work through the variety of different kinds of questions, rather than concentrating on just one kind.

- **Questions which test your knowledge and understanding of facts** – for these questions, you have to give information, perhaps about the beliefs of the religion you have been studying, or perhaps about the place of worship, the work of a charity, a festival or some other topic. You need to show that you understand the information you are giving by explaining its importance to religious believers.

- **Questions which test your understanding of how religious belief affects people's lives** – these questions ask you to show that you understand the effects of a religion on its members – for example, showing how beliefs affect behaviour or how a religious believer might feel about something.

- **Questions which test your ability to evaluate** – these questions ask for your opinion and the opinions of religious believers. You need to practise giving your reasons as well as just saying what you think. Think about explaining how a religious believer might answer the question and show you understand their reasons.

Check your written answers with the examples given in the book and on the video. You might find it useful to get a friend to mark it for you, while you mark theirs. Talk about how your answers are different, and why you think one answer is better than the other.

Even if you have finished having lessons and are on study leave, you could write practice answers and take them into school to show to your teacher and ask for comments. Check first that your teacher will be available on the day and at the time that you plan to visit!

On the day

Make sure that you get to bed at a reasonable time the night before an exam and don't try to stay up too late to revise. Ask someone to check that you don't oversleep and remember to eat a proper breakfast. Take two or three blue or black pens with you (don't use other colours) and allow yourself plenty of time to get to the exam.

If your exam paper is divided into sections, make sure that you know which sections you have been prepared for. Make sure that you know how long the exam will last, how many questions you have to answer and whether any of them are compulsory. Divide your time carefully and make sure that you spend the most time on the questions that are worth the most marks. Jot down a few notes (not too many) as a plan for each answer before you start to write. If you can't think of anything to write in your notes, you've still got time to choose a different question!

Read the questions carefully and make sure you understand what you are being asked to do. If you are unsure of an answer, write something, even if it states the obvious, but never leave an answer blank – you cannot be given any marks for writing nothing.

Remember – the examiners want to see how much you can do and are not trying to catch you out! They will try and give you marks wherever they can.

REMEMBER Throughout this book, where dates are referred to, the abbreviation BCE (Before Common Era) is used instead of BC (Before Christ), and CE (Common Era) instead of AD (Anno Domini).

Good luck!

Buddhism

To answer questions on the following topics, you need to know about:

Buddhist beliefs

- what Buddhists believe about their religion
- how Buddhists show these beliefs in their daily lives.

This section focuses on what Buddhists believe and why. You will have the opportunity to answer a question about particular Buddhist beliefs.

Buddhist holy books

- what the Buddhist holy books are and what they contain
- the use which Buddhists make of these books in their lives and worship.

You will have the opportunity to answer a question about the use which people make of their holy books in their daily lives.

Buddhist festivals

- what the main Buddhist festivals are
- what particular events or stories the festivals are celebrating
- how they are celebrated.

This section focuses on some of the main festivals of Buddhism. It also gives you the opportunity to practise answering questions about different points of view.

Buddhist rites of passage

- the Buddhist rites of passage
- how these are celebrated and why they are important.

You need to remember that not all Buddhists celebrate these rites of passage in the same way. You will also have the opportunity to answer a question about rites of passage for which you need to consider different points of view.

Buddhist pilgrimage

- Buddhist teaching about pilgrimage
- some places of Buddhist pilgrimage
- why Buddhists might decide to go on a pilgrimage
- what effect a pilgrimage might have on Buddhists' lives after they return home.

In this section, you will have the opportunity to answer a question on the reasons people go on pilgrimages and the effect that this might have on them.

Buddhist places of worship

- the main features of Buddhist places of worship and the reasons for their design
- the principal forms of worship which take place in these buildings.

At the end of this section, you will be given the opportunity to answer a question about the purpose of Buddhist worship.

Buddhist beliefs

All religions are about believing in certain things. Buddhists follow the teachings of the Buddha, Siddatha Gotama.

Some Buddhists prefer not to describe their beliefs as a religion.

Buddhism teaches a life which avoids extremes. Buddhists try to live according to the 'Middle Way'. In this way, they hope to escape from the cycle of birth and rebirth.

There is no god or supreme deity in Buddhism.

Buddhist holy books

There are many Buddhist holy books. These books include the Theravada texts, such as the Pali canon and the Tipitaka, and the Mahayana texts, which include the Pranjapamita and Lotus Sutras.

For four centuries, these books were passed down orally.

Buddhist festivals

Most Buddhist festivals centre on the religious Sangha, Bhikkhus (monks) and Bhikkhunis (nuns).

Festivals are not required by the Buddhist scriptures.

Some of the main festivals of the Buddhist year are:

- Uposatha Days – weekly festivals
- Rains Retreat
- Wesak
- New Year.

It is important to remember that festivals may be celebrated very differently in different parts of the world.

Buddhist rites of passage

The four main rites of passage for Buddhists are:

- birth
- samanera – a coming of age event
- marriage – the blessing of two people who intend to spend the rest of their lives together
- death – the ceremonies when a person dies.

It is very important to remember that birth and marriage do not have specific Buddhist ceremonies associated with them.

Buddhist pilgrimage

Pilgrimages are not holidays. Pilgrimage isn't an obligation for Buddhists but many Buddhists try to visit places associated with their faith.

Giving up time to go on a pilgrimage might help to strengthen a Buddhist's faith.

Buddhist places of worship

Buddhists pray and meditate in a temple or shrine and at home.

Buddhist temples are designed to symbolise the beliefs of Buddhists and to help them in their worship.

Buddhist beliefs

The Buddha

Buddhism began in India about 2500 years ago. It teaches a way of life that avoids extremes, shunning both self-indulgence and self-denial. There is no god or supreme deity. Buddhism's beliefs and practices are based on the teachings of the **Buddha**, Siddatha Gotama, who gave up his family and possessions to live an ascetic life in order to search for enlightenment.

The teachings of the Buddha are **dhamma** (universal truth). The Buddha taught the 'Middle Way'. Craving and desire keep people on the wheel, the cycle of birth and rebirth. Only enlightenment can help people escape this. In order to achieve enlightenment, Buddhists follow the Four Noble Truths:

Dukkha: suffering – all humans suffer since the pleasures of life do not last.
Samudaya: desire or craving for things.
Nirodha: the removal of dukkha.
Magga: how to remove dukkha – by following magga – the Noble Eightfold Path, which comprises:

- right view or right understanding
- right thought
- right speech
- right action
- right way of life
- right effort
- right mindfulness
- right concentration.

! REMEMBER Buddhists follow the teachings of the Buddha but they do not worship him as a god.

By following the Eightfold Path, Buddhists hope to achieve **nibbana** – the destruction of all their bad **karma** (results of their actions) and so instead of being reborn, they reach parinibbana (complete nibbana).

All Buddhist should live by the Five Precepts, refraining from:
- destroying life
- taking what is not given
- impurity
- lying
- using intoxicating substances.

In addition, Buddhist monks (the monastic **Sangha**) follow a further five precepts:
- not eating at inappropriate times
- not indulging in singing and dancing
- not wearing garlands, perfumes or other ornaments
- not sleeping in a high or broad bed
- not receiving gold or silver.

Practice question

- Explain why the teachings of the Buddha are still so important to Buddhists today.

Practise writing one or two paragraphs in answer to this question. You need to consider why these beliefs are important, as well as the effect they might have on the life of a Buddhist.

Buddhist holy books

Texts from the Buddhist scriptures are sometimes used as prayers or for meditation. Others are studied in order to understand Buddhism and help individuals in their search for enlightenment.

The Buddha died when he was eighty and his followers passed on his teachings orally. A council was held in 480BCE in Ragir to agree on a text as followers realised that oral teachings could be changed by repetition. A further council in 380BCE caused a split within Buddhism.

Theravadan scriptures

After the split, one of the groups became known as **Theravada** Buddhists (the Way of the Elders or the Lesser Vehicle). They spread south through Sri Lanka and to Thailand. The first Buddhist scriptures were probably written down by Theravadan monks in the first century BCE.

Pali canon – Tipitaka – the three baskets

The names above are given to the following group of three books:

Vinaya Pitaka: this contains the rules for the Sangha, the Four Noble Truths and the Eightfold Path.

Sutta Pitaka: this contains the stories of the Buddha's life and enlightenment and some of the basic philosophies and doctrines of Buddhism.

Abhidhamma Pitaka: this contains the philosophy of Buddhist teachings.

Mahayana scriptures

Mahayana Buddhism is known as the Vehicle. It spread northwards into China, Japan and Tibet. The Mahayana scriptures include:

Pranjaparamita Sutras: written in Sanskrit between 100BCE and 600CE, these are a guide to achieving the wisdom of the Bodhisattva – wisdom which goes beyond the world. They also includes the Diamond Sutra and the Heart Sutra.

The Lotus Sutra: the final teachings of the Buddha.

> **❶ REMEMBER**
> There are different groups of Buddhists who have different beliefs and ways of worshipping.

Practice question

■ Explain why the teachings of the Buddhist scriptures are still important today and how they might affect the way people live.

Practise writing one or two paragraphs in answer to this question. You need to consider more than one of the scriptures and explain the importance which Buddhists give to them. You also need to mention how teachings from them might influence people's daily lives.

Buddhist festivals

Buddhist monks receiving alms

Uposatha days

This is a weekly monastic festival which is held on each quarter of the moon. In Theravada communities, lay people may stay at a monastery for all, or part of, the day. In Mahayana communities, some lay Buddhists will make offerings (usually of food) to monks and visit Buddhist shrines.

Rains Retreat

During the monsoon season (from July to September) in northern India, Theravada monks settled in one place. Most monks returned from the countryside to their monasteries during this time.

The Kathina Ceremony

At the end of the Rains Retreat, lay Buddhists present monks with new robes.

❗ REMEMBER Buddhist festivals are often different according to the part of the world in which Buddhism is being practised. If you are answering a question about Buddhist festivals, you must show that you are aware of this.

Wesak

Wesak celebrates the Buddha's birth, enlightenment and death, which all took place on the same day of the year. It is probably the most important of all Buddhist festivals. Celebrations are very different from one country to another. Temples are decorated and Wesak lanterns, made of thin paper stuck over a wooden frame, are hung up. People send Wesak cards to each other and visit monasteries to give food to the monks.

New Year

This is not a religious festival, although it is widely celebrated. It includes Chinese New Year, and the Tibetan New Year when the country is rededicated to Buddhism. In Sri Lanka, people visit the Temple of the Buddha's Tooth in Kandy.

Practice question

■ Do you agree that it is important to celebrate festivals every year?

Practise writing one or two paragraphs in answer to this question. In your answer, you should look at different opinions. You also need to think carefully about what effect celebrating festivals regularly might have on the life of a Buddhist. You might argue that they lose their meaning if you celebrate them too often.

Buddhist rites of passage

Birth

Buddhists do not have a ceremony to mark the birth of a child, but they may follow local customs. They believe that everyone is reincarnated from a previous existence and so could be influenced by bad karma. Parents bring their children up to follow the teachings of the Buddha.

Samanera

In some Buddhist countries, as a coming of age event, boys enter a monastery for a short period of time as Samanera. They are treated as novices and help with the running of the monastery. This lower ordination takes place when the boys are between eight and twenty. The Samanera follow the additional Five Precepts of the monastic **Sangha** (see page 12).

Marriage

Marriage and family life are very important to lay Buddhists but there is no religious ceremony to mark marriage. People are usually married with some form of registry office ceremony and then go to a monastery where they offer food and ask the Sangha (religious community) for a blessing.

Death

When a Buddhist dies, the corpse is washed, placed in a coffin and covered with flowers. The coffin is taken to the nearest Sangha or shrine. Offerings of food and flowers are made. The ceremonies which take place vary widely, but because death brings a person closer to **nibbana**, some events are more to do with celebration than mourning. The corpses are usually cremated and the ashes are then scattered into a river or the sea.

! REMEMBER When you are writing about Buddhism, you must try to see how a Buddhist would feel about a particular idea or situation.

Practice question

■ 'You cannot take on adult responsibilities in your religion when you are a teenager.' Do you agree?

Practise writing one or two paragraphs in answer to this question. In your answer, you need to be sensitive to what Buddhists might think about this issue. Remember to show that you understand different views about what it means to be an adult. Think about whether religious teachings should have priority when making this sort of decision.

Buddhist pilgrimage

Four pilgrimage sites are associated with the life of the Buddha. They are:

Lumbini Grove, Nepal

This is the site of the Buddha's birth. A stone pillar built by King Ashoka commemorates the event.

Bodh Gaya, Bihar

This is the place where the Buddha attained enlightenment. The Bodhi tree is a descendant of the original under which the Buddha sat. A stone beside the tree is said to bear the Buddha's footprint. Pilgrims take flags and garlands of flowers to decorate the tree.

The Deer Park, Sarnath

This is at Varanasi where the Buddha preached his first sermon. The park has a large stupa built by King Ashoka.

Kushinara (Kaisa)

This is traditionally believed to be the place of the Buddha's death.

Other places of pilgrimage

Many pilgrims also visit temples and stupas. Stupas were originally built over relics of the Buddha. Sometimes, they contain other sacred objects. People are not allowed inside stupas.

REMEMBER
When you are answering questions about pilgrimage, it's important to think about the effect a pilgrimage might have on someone after he or she returns to normal life.

Practice question

■ Choose one place of pilgrimage, explain why it's important for Buddhists and the effect which a visit to this place may have when they return home.

Practise writing one or two paragraphs in answer to this question. It is important to answer all parts of the question. You need to explain why the place you have chosen is important for Buddhists and what they might do there. You also need to consider the effect which the visit might have on their everyday lives after they return home.

Buddhist places of worship

The temple

Buddhists do not worship a god. They work towards enlightenment and honour the Buddha who showed them the way. When Buddhists pray, they are praying to the Buddha within themselves.

In Buddhist countries, there are many temples where people can make offerings. In other countries, most worship takes place at a shrine in the home. Temples are mostly found in the **Theravada** tradition. They contain living quarters for the monks, an area for the monks to worship and a shrine with images of the Buddha and an altar for offerings. There will also be a preaching area where monks can deliver sermons.

Daily worship

Whether in a home, temple or monastery, daily worship takes place in the same way. Worshippers take off their shoes, put their hands together and walk towards the image of the Buddha. They make offerings of flowers, light and incense. They then recite the Three Refuges –

I go to the Buddha for Refuge.
I go to the Doctrine for Refuge.
I go to the Order for Refuge.

– and then the Five Precepts (see page 12).

A central feature of Buddhist worship is meditation. The traditional way to meditate is to sit cross-legged in the lotus position with the right hand on top of the left. People sit quietly and try to clear their minds of all thoughts.

Samatha meditation: Samatha means 'the path of concentration'. The worshipper tries to remove all distractions by concentrating on a single object. Buddhist scriptures say that there are eight different jhanas (states of consciousness) which can be reached.

Vipassana meditation: this type of meditation involves thinking deeply about the teachings of Buddhism, such as the Four Noble Truths and the Eightfold Path.

Zazen – Zen meditation: this form of meditation takes place with the eyes open, looking at an object such as a specially designed Zen garden.

> **! REMEMBER**
> When you are answering a question about Buddhist worship, remember that the most important part of Buddhist worship is meditation, when people pray to the Buddha within themselves.

Practice question

■ Explain the meaning and purpose of Buddhist worship.

Practise writing one or two paragraphs in answer to this question. Although you need to describe Buddhist worship, remember to 'explain its meaning and purpose' and how it relates to Buddhist beliefs.

To answer questions on the following topics, you need to know about:

Christian beliefs

- what Christians believe about their God and their religion
- how Christians show these beliefs in their daily lives.

This section focuses on what Christians believe and why. You will have the opportunity to answer a question about particular Christian beliefs.

Christian holy books

- what the Christian holy books are and what they contain
- the use which Christians make of these books in their lives and worship.

This section deals with the Christian Bible, what it contains and the ways in which Christians use it today. You will have the opportunity to answer a question about how people use the Bible in their daily lives.

Christian festivals

- what the main Christian festivals are
- what particular events the festivals are celebrating
- how they are celebrated.

This section focuses on the main festivals of the Christian Church. It gives you the opportunity to answer a question about different points of view.

Christian rites of passage

- the four Christian rites of passage
- how these are celebrated and why they are important.

You need to remember that not all Christians celebrate these rites of passage in the same way. You will have the opportunity to answer a question about rites of passage for which you need to consider different points of view.

Christian pilgrimage

- some places of Christian pilgrimage
- why Christians might decide to go on a pilgrimage
- what effect a pilgrimage might have on a person's life after he or she returns home.

In this section, you will have the opportunity to answer a question on the reasons people go on pilgrimages and the effect this might have on them.

Christian places of worship

- the main Christian denominations and how their traditions have influenced the buildings they use for worship
- the main features of Christian places of worship and the reasons for the design
- the principal forms of worship which take place in these buildings.

You will be given the opportunity to answer a question about the reasons for the design of a particular place of Christian worship.

Christian beliefs

All religions are about believing in certain things. Christianity is about a belief in one God who has three 'persons' or 'natures': God the Father, God the Son (Jesus) and God the Holy Spirit. These three together are called the Trinity.

Christians believe that they should follow the teachings of Jesus and live their lives according to his example.

There are over 25 000 different denominations (branches) of Christianity.

Christian holy books

The Christian scriptures, which are the Old and the New Testaments, are called the Bible.

In the Old Testament, there are 39 books - the Jewish Bible (the Tenakh).

The New Testament contains 27 books which were probably all written during the first hundred years after the death of Jesus. The New Testament contains Christian teachings about the life and death of Jesus, and what it means to be a Christian.

Christian festivals

The main festivals of the Christian calendar follow Jesus' life according to the gospels.

- Advent – the four weeks before the birth of Jesus
- Christmas – celebrates the birth of Jesus (25 December)
- Epiphany – the visit of the wise men and the gifts they brought to Jesus (6 January)
- Lent – the six weeks before Easter
- Palm Sunday – the Sunday before Easter when Jesus entered Jerusalem
- Easter – the most important Christian festival which remembers the death and resurrection of Jesus

- Ascension Day – forty days after Easter when Jesus ascended into heaven
- Pentecost (Whitsun) – ten days after the Ascension when the Holy Spirit came to Jesus' disciples.

Christian rites of passage

The four rites of passage for Christians are:

- baptism – this marks entry into the Church
- confirmation – the acceptance of Christ by a teenager or adult
- marriage – the Church blessing two people who intend to spend the rest of their lives together
- death – the ceremonies when a person dies and hopes to go to heaven.

Christian pilgrimage

Pilgrimages are not holidays. Giving up time to go on a pilgrimage might help to strengthen a Christian's faith.

There are many places of pilgrimage in the Holy Land. Many people also go on pilgrimages to places such as Lourdes, where healing miracles are believed to take place.

Roman Catholics may go to Rome on pilgrimage to Vatican City, the centre of the Roman Catholic Church and the home of the Pope, the head of the Roman Catholic Church.

Christian places of worship

Most Christians worship in a church. Churches are designed to symbolise Christian beliefs and to help Christians in their worship.

The different designs of buildings used for worship often reflect the beliefs and views of a particular denomination. Therefore, some churches are very elaborate and highly decorated inside whilst others are very plain.

The design of a church can also reflect the type of worship which takes place there.

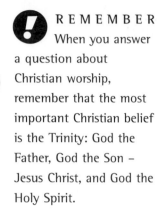

🖳 Christian beliefs

REMEMBER
When you answer a question about Christian worship, remember that the most important Christian belief is the Trinity: God the Father, God the Son – Jesus Christ, and God the Holy Spirit.

The central beliefs of Christianity are found in the Bible. The life and teachings of Jesus of Nazareth, often called **Jesus Christ**, are found in the **New Testament** of the Bible (see page 21).

Christians believe that Jesus is the son of God. He was born as a human so 'God became Man' – this is called the Incarnation. He lived on Earth, in what is now Israel, from about 4BCE to 30CE. He spent three years of his adult life preaching around Galilee and in Jerusalem. He was tried for blasphemy by the leaders of the Jewish Temple and by the Romans who governed the country. He was found guilty and crucified. His death was the ultimate sacrifice for humanity. He rose from the dead after three days.

Christians believe that Jesus' death atoned for all the **sin** in the world and that, because of this, followers of Jesus have eternal life. Jesus said, '*I am the resurrection and the life. Those who believe in me, even though they die, will live, and everyone who lives and believes in me will never die.*' (John 11:25-26)

Christians follow the example of Jesus and his teachings in their daily lives. In particular, they follow the teachings of the Sermon on the Mount (Matthew 5-7). They achieve salvation by their belief in Jesus – 'salvation by faith'. When people commit sin, their relationship with God is broken and they need to ask for forgiveness.

Christians believe that they are helped in their daily lives by praying to Jesus and by the influence and guidance of the **Holy Spirit**. The main beliefs of Christianity are contained in statements of belief called **creeds**. A well-known one, often recited in churches, is the Apostles' Creed.

The Apostles' Creed
I believe in God, the Father almighty, creator of heaven and earth.
I believe in Jesus Christ, his only son, our Lord.
He was conceived by the power of the Holy Spirit, and born of the Virgin Mary.
He suffered under Pontius Pilate, was crucified, died and was buried.
He descended to the dead.
On the third day he rose again.
He ascended into heaven, and is seated at the right hand of the Father.
He will come again to judge the living and the dead.
I believe in the Holy Spirit, the holy catholic church, the communion of saints, the forgiveness of sins, the resurrection of the body, and the life everlasting.

Practice question

■ Explain what Christians mean when they say that Jesus is God's son.

Practise writing one or two paragraphs in answer to this question. Remember that for high marks you will need to explain something about Jesus' life and death as well as writing about the Christian belief in the Trinity.

Christian holy books

Old Testament (39 books)

Jesus was a Jew, as were his first followers. For this reason, the **Old Testament** is a very important part of the Bible. It contains history, law, poetry and prophecy. One of its major themes is the relationship between God and humanity. The prophets wrote about the coming of a Messiah, who would bring peace to the earth. Isaiah wrote about a Servant of God who would suffer for the people's sins. Christians believe this servant was Jesus.

REMEMBER Jesus was a Jew and so were most of the disciples.

New Testament (27 books)

The Gospels (the 'good news' about Jesus). There are four gospels: Matthew, Mark, Luke and John. They are accounts of Jesus' life on Earth, from his birth to his final ascension into **heaven**. They are named after the people who are thought to have written them. The accounts in them sometimes differ slightly.

Acts The next book is the Acts of the Apostles which tells the story of the early church and the first Christians.

Epistles There are 21 epistles (letters), some written by the apostle Paul, designed to teach and support the early Christians across the Mediterranean.

Revelation The last book in the Bible, the Book of Revelation, contains prophecies about the Day of Judgement.

Some Christians believe that every word of the Bible is exactly as God wanted it to be and that it is a 'revealed' book. Other Christians think that although it was inspired by God, as it was written down by people there may be some mistakes in it.

The Bible is used in worship and in Christians' daily lives. It usually has a special place of importance in a **church**. It is often kept on a stand called a lectern. Readings from the Bible are a very important part of all services. During the **eucharist** or **Holy Communion**, there are often three readings: one each from the Old Testament, the Epistles or the book of Revelation, and from the Gospels. Sermons are often based on the theme of the readings.

Many Christians read the Bible at home every day and some Christian families read passages together. Christians believe that the Bible contains the teachings they need to understand God and follow Jesus' teachings.

Practice question

■ Explain how Christians might use the Bible to make decisions about how they should live.

Practise writing one or two paragraphs in answer to this question. Note that you are not being asked to describe the Bible but you do need to say why it is so important to Christians. In particular, consider how individual Christians might use biblical teachings when they face difficult decisions.

Christian festivals

REMEMBER
When you are writing about Christianity, you must try to see how a Christian would feel about a particular idea or situation.

Christmas

The account of the birth of Jesus is found in Matthew and Luke. The accounts are slightly different. The story is about a young woman called Mary who was engaged to a man called Joseph. She was visited by an angel who told her she was pregnant by the Holy Spirit. She gave birth to a baby, Jesus, in a stable in Bethlehem, near Jerusalem. The baby was visited by shepherds who had been told to go to Bethlehem by angels, and later by wise men who had followed a star and who brought gifts of gold, frankincense and myrrh.

On Christmas Day, special church services celebrate Jesus' birth. People give each other presents, eat special Christmas meals and decorate their houses with Christmas trees, lights and holly.

REMEMBER
When you are answering questions about Christian festivals, don't forget that Easter Day is the most important of all because it remembers the time when Jesus overcame death.

Easter

The week before **Easter** is called **Holy Week**. On **Palm Sunday**, some churches have processions around the streets and people carry palm crosses to remember Jesus' arrival in Jerusalem. On the Thursday of Holy Week, **Maundy Thursday**, Christians remember the last meal which Jesus had with his disciples. In many churches, special services are held. Sometimes, people's feet are washed by a priest in the same way that Jesus washed his disciples' feet. The service also remembers the Last Supper, the very first **eucharist**. **Good Friday** marks the death of Jesus on the cross and many churches hold solemn services from 12 noon until 3pm – the time during which Jesus was crucified.

Easter Day is the happiest event of the Christian year because Christians are remembering Jesus' rising from the dead. Churches are decorated and many people give each other Easter eggs which symbolise new life.

Ascension Day recalls the occasion when Jesus was with his disciples for the last time and then ascended into **Heaven**. The story of **Pentecost** (Whitsun) can be found in Acts 2:1-4. All the disciples were together when wind swept through the room and flames of fire touched their heads. This was the **Holy Spirit**. Afterwards, the disciples found they could speak in many languages and tell people about Jesus.

Practice question

■ Do you agree that Christmas has become so commercialised that people have completely forgotten what it is about?

Practise writing one or two paragraphs in answer to this question. In this question, you have to look at different opinions. You need to think carefully about the real meaning of Christmas and decide whether all the commercialism helps the celebration of Jesus' birth or whether the importance becomes lost.

Christian rites of passage

📺 Baptism

Christians believe that when Adam and Eve disobeyed God in the Garden of Eden, they brought **sin** into the world. All people are born with original sin (the tendency to do wrong rather than right) because of this. Baptism is a sign that this sin has been washed away. Baptism usually takes place as soon after birth as possible. The priest marks a cross on the baby's head with water from the font. The baby is named and blessed. In some churches, such as the Baptist Church, people are baptised as adults, generally by immersion.

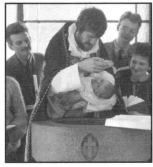

An Anglican baptism

Confirmation

Confirmation is the ceremony at which Christians reaffirm their infant baptism vows. At a special service, they kneel in front of a Bishop who places his hands on their heads and prays that they will receive the Holy Spirit.

Marriage

Christians want to have their marriage blessed by God. The ceremony usually takes place in a **church**. The couple exchange rings and make public vows to each other which include loving and looking after one another and being faithful. Many Christians do not agree with divorce because they believe that marriage vows are made to God and so cannot be broken.

> **❗ REMEMBER**
> All Christian rites of passage are religious events which take place before God in worship.

Death

Christians believe that when Jesus came back from the dead, he overcame the power of death. Therefore, they do not think that death is the end. The soul of the person lives on and is united with God. Christians are buried or cremated. A funeral service takes place and this is followed by burial in a graveyard or cemetery or by a cremation with the burial of the ashes. When the coffin or ashes are placed in the ground, the priest says, 'We commit this body to the ground, earth to earth, ashes to ashes, dust to dust'. Relatives will often place flowers on the grave and a stone will mark the grave.

> **❗ REMEMBER**
> Christians do not believe in reincarnation.

Practice question

■ 'Religion is a personal thing and people should make decisions for themselves. Therefore, it is wrong to baptise babies.' Do you agree?

Practise writing one or two paragraphs in answer to this question. In your answer, you need to be sensitive to what Christians might think about this issue. You need to show that you understand different Christian views about infant baptism as well as explaining what baptism is about and why it is important.

Christian pilgrimage

Although Christians do not have to go on pilgrimage as part of their religion, there are many places which attract pilgrims.

The Holy Land

Bethlehem
This is Jesus' birth place. The Church of the Nativity stands on the traditional site of the stable and was originally built by the Roman Emperor Constantine.

Nazareth
Jesus grew up in Nazareth and lived there for the first thirty years of his life. There are several churches on different sites and each of them claims to be the site of the Annunciation – when Mary was visited by the Archangel Gabriel and told that she would give birth to Jesus, God's son.

Jerusalem
Jesus lived in Jerusalem during the last days of his life – he was tried and put to death there. Pilgrims visit the Via Dolorosa where Jesus carried his cross. They also go to churches on the traditional sites of Jesus' crucifixion, the tomb where he was buried and the hill from where he ascended to heaven.

Other places of pilgrimage

Rome – Vatican City
Pilgrims visit the Basilica of Saint Peter where Saint Peter is said to be buried. They may also visit the church of Saint Paul Ante Lateran where the apostle Paul is believed to be buried. Pilgrims often visit Rome at Easter to hear the Pope's Easter message and may also try to go there during a Holy Year.

Lourdes
In 1858, a young girl called Marie Bernarde Soubirous (Saint Bernadette) had a vision of the Virgin Mary in a grotto at Lourdes. Today, many pilgrims visit Lourdes, hoping for a cure. There are 64 reported cures that have been declared 'miracles'. Many other people have found that visiting Lourdes, although not curing them, has given them strength to fight their illness.

Practice question

■ Choose one place of pilgrimage and explain why it is important to Christians. Discuss how a visit to this place may help them when they return home.

Practise writing one or two paragraphs in answer to this question. It is important to answer all parts of the question. You will need to explain why the place you have chosen is important for Christians and what they might do there. You also need to consider the effect this visit might have on their everyday life after they return home.

Christian places of worship

The church

Roman Catholic churches
Roman Catholic churches are often built in a cruciform (cross) shape, with the head of the cross facing east, towards Jerusalem. They have stained glass windows illustrating stories from the Bible or the lives of the saints. On the walls are fourteen paintings or carvings representing the Stations of the Cross – important events in the last hours leading up to Jesus' crucifixion.

Near the door is the **font** where **baptisms** take place and people 'enter' the church. At the east end is the chancel. Here, you usually find the **pulpit**, from which sermons are preached, and the lectern, which holds the Bible. At the east end of the chancel is the sanctuary. Here is the **altar**, a stone or wooden table where the bread and wine is prepared for the **eucharist**. There may be a cross or crucifix and candles on the altar. There may be another altar at the 'crossing', where the nave and the chancel meet.

Anglican churches
These are usually very similar to Roman Catholic churches in their design, although often they are plainer. The eucharist is usually the main service.

Orthodox churches
Orthodox churches are similar in many ways to Roman Catholic churches but there are no seats for the congregation, and the chancel and sanctuary are behind a screen called an iconostasis. The iconostasis is decorated with icons (paintings) of Jesus and the saints and in the centre are the Royal Doors which are opened and closed during the services.

Baptist churches or chapels
These are often very plain buildings. A central pulpit emphasises that the Bible and preaching are at the centre of Baptist worship. In front of the pulpit is a covered tank in which believers are immersed during baptism.

Quaker meeting house (Religious Society of Friends)
These are extremely plain buildings containing chairs placed around a table on which there is sometimes a Bible. In Quaker services, people sit in silence until someone feels moved to speak.

> **! REMEMBER**
> For the majority of Christians, and especially for Roman Catholics, the eucharist is the most important service.

> **! REMEMBER**
> Modern churches are built according to a variety of designs. Many now place the altar in the middle of the congregation.

Practice question

■ Choose one Christian place of worship and explain the meaning and symbolism of its features and furnishings.

Practise writing one or two paragraphs in answer to this question. Although you will need to describe the features and furnishings of the building, you must remember to explain what they are used for and the Christian beliefs associated with them.

To answer questions on the following topics, you need to know about:

Hindu beliefs

- what Hindus believe about their God and their religion
- how Hindus show these beliefs in their daily lives.

This section focuses on what Hindus believe and why. You will have the opportunity to answer a question about particular Hindu beliefs.

Hindu holy books

- what the Hindu holy books are and what they contain
- the use which Hindus make of these books in their lives and worship.

You will have the opportunity to answer a question about the use which people make of their holy books in their daily lives.

Hindu festivals

- what the main Hindu festivals are
- what particular events or stories the festivals are celebrating
- how they are celebrated.

This section focuses on the main festivals of Hinduism. It also gives you the opportunity to practise answering questions about different points of view.

Hindu rites of passage

- the four main Hindu rites of passage
- how these are celebrated and why they are important.

You need to remember that not all Hindus celebrate these rites of passage in the same way. You will also have the opportunity to answer a question about rites of passage for which you need to consider different points of view.

Hindu pilgrimage

- Hindu teaching about pilgrimage
- some places of Hindu pilgrimage
- why Hindus might decide to go on a pilgrimage
- what effect a pilgrimage might have on people's lives after they return home.

In this section, you will have the opportunity to answer a question on the reasons people go on pilgrimages and the effects this might have on them.

Hindu places of worship

- the main features of Hindu places of worship and the reasons for their design
- the principal forms of worship which take place in these buildings.

At the end of this section, you will be given the opportunity to answer a question about the reasons for the design of a mandir.

Hindu beliefs

All religions are about believing in certain things. Hindus try to live according to their dharma (duty) in the hope of reaching moksha (final release from the cycle of rebirth).

There is a wide variety of belief and practice in Hinduism.

Hindu holy books

There are many Hindu holy books. These books include the Vedas, the Upanishads, the Puranas, the Tantras, the Laws of Manu, the Ramayana and the Mahabharata.

They are divided into two main categories – Shruti and Smriti.

Some Hindu holy books are among the oldest writings in existence.

Hindu festivals

These are some of main festivals of the Hindu year:

- Divali
- Holi
- Janmashtami
- Raksha Bandhan.

It is important to remember that festivals may be celebrated very differently in different parts of India and by Hindus who come from particular areas.

Hindu rites of passage

The four main rites of passage for Hindus are:

- birth
- Uppanayana – the sacred thread ceremony
- marriage – the blessing of two people who intend to spend the rest of their lives together
- death – the ceremonies when a person dies.

Hindu pilgrimage

Pilgrimages are not holidays. Many places in India are sacred to Hindus – some to particular sects or groups.

Pilgrimage is an act of religious devotion and, for many people, it is part of the search for moksha.

Giving up time to go on a pilgrimage might help to strengthen a Hindu's faith.

Pilgrimage often involves hardship and personal sacrifice.

Hindu places of worship

Hindus worship in a mandir and at home.

Mandirs are designed to symbolise the beliefs of Hindus and to help them in their worship.

Hinduism

Hindu beliefs

28

REMEMBER The most important Hindu belief is the Ultimate Reality – Brahman, who is the Supreme Spirit of the universe.

Hindus believe that there is one Ultimate Reality – **Brahman** – the Supreme Spirit of the universe. Brahman has three main functions and these are portrayed by the three gods:

- **Shiva** – the Destroyer, because change is necessary for the creation of new things
- **Brahma** – the Creator and source of all creation
- **Vishnu** – the Preserver.

Vishnu has ten main **avatars** (incarnations). These represent the times when Vishnu came to Earth to overcome evil. The most popular avatars of Vishnu are Rama and Krishna. There are many other gods in Hinduism, both male and female. All of these represent different attributes and strengths. One of the most popular is **Ganesha**, the elephant-headed god of good fortune.

REMEMBER When you are answering a question about Hindu beliefs, remember that the aim of all Hindus is to reach moksha.

Hindus believe that every action has an effect and there is a cause for everything that happens in life. This is the law of **karma**. After a person's death, their **atman** (or soul) lives on and takes on a new life in another body. This is called reincarnation. Karma affects a person's future life. The whole cycle of birth and rebirth is called **samsara**. Liberation from samsara – which is **moksha** – is the ultimate aim of all Hindus.

Varnashrama is the belief that life is divided into four varnas (groups) and four ashramas (stages). **Dharma** is the code of conduct that a Hindu must follow. Hindu society is divided into four varnas:

- Brahmin – teacher or priest
- Kshatriya – ruler or warrior
- Vaishya – merchant or farmer
- Sudra – servant or labourer.

There are four ashramas (stages) of life which are ideals through which people may pass. These are:

- Brahmacharya ashrama – the student
- Grihastha ashrama – the householder
- Vanprastha ashrama – the hermit
- Sannyasa ashrama – the wandering holy man.

Practice question

- Explain why beliefs about Varnashrama are still so important to Hindus today.

Practise writing one or two paragraphs in answer to this question. You need to consider why these beliefs are important, as well as the effect which they might have on the life of a Hindu.

Hindu holy books

The Hindu scriptures

The Hindu scriptures are divided into two main categories:

Shruti: Shruti means 'what was heard'. These writings were handed down from the gods. They include the Vedas and Upanishads.

Smriti: Smriti means 'what was remembered'. These writings were handed down by tradition. They include the later scriptures, such as the Tantras and the Puranas.

The Hindu scriptures consist of the following books:

Vedas (including the Upanishads): these were written between 1200BCE-600BCE. The most important is the Rig Veda – a collection of 1028 hymns written in praise of the Vedic gods such as Agni (the god of fire) and Indra (the storm god). The Upanishads are about the relationship between atman and Brahman (see page 28).

Great Epics (Ramayana and Mahabharata): these were written between 400BCE-50BCE. They are very long epic poems about the gods. The Ramayana contain the stories of Rama and Sita. The last eighteen chapters of the Mahabharata form the Bhagavad Gita, the best known of the Hindu scriptures.

Puranas: these were written between 300CE-650CE. They are a collection of stories about the lives of avatars and saints.

Tantras: written between 650CE-1000CE, these are about Shakti, the female aspect of power and creation.

Manu Smriti – the laws of Manu: written between 600CE-300CE, these are rules which govern everyday life.

Hindu priests are trained to read the scriptures in Sanskrit. Indian holy men, especially the **gurus**, give talks and lectures explaining the religious teachings to people who go to learn from them. The epics, such as the Mahabharata and the Ramayana, are very popular with Hindus today and the stories from them are often represented in comic strip format as well as appearing on television.

> **! REMEMBER**
> The Hindu scriptures were written over many thousands of years and are written in Sanskrit which people have to learn to read.

29

Hinduism

Practice question

■ Explain why the teachings of the Hindu scriptures are still important today and how they might affect the way people live.

Practise writing one or two paragraphs in answer to this question. In your answer, you need to consider more than one of the scriptures. Remember to explain the importance which Hindus attach to them and how teachings from them might influence people's daily lives.

BITESIZEreligious education

Hindu festivals

! REMEMBER
Different Hindu communities emphasise different stories and festivals.

Divali

The name 'Divali' comes from the Sanskrit 'dipavali' and means 'group of lights'. This five-day festival takes place at the end of autumn during the month of Karttika. The festival remembers the return of King Rama to his kingdom after fourteen years of exile. It is also a celebration of Lakshmi Puja to welcome the goddess of good fortune. People put divas (small clay lamps) in windows, wear new clothes, send cards and exchange sweets or presents.

Holi

Holi is celebrated at the full moon in February or March. It was originally a northern Indian festival. The festival originates with Krishna who, as a young boy, threw coloured water over the gopis (milkmaids). It is also thought that a demon tried to kill the baby Krishna by giving him poisoned milk. Krishna turned blue but did not die and the demon shrivelled to ashes. At Holi, people throw coloured powder or water at each other, bonfires are lit and parents carry their babies with them to protect them from the demons.

Janmashtami

This is the birthday of Lord Krishna on the eighth day of Bhadrapada (August/September). People decorate their homes with lights and tinsel. Singing lasts until midnight and then a special **puja** is performed. In the **mandirs**, there is a cradle for Krishna. At midnight, the curtains are drawn back and people rock the baby Krishna in his cradle. The festival remembers that Krishna's father had to flee with him to save Krishna from being killed by a wicked relative.

! REMEMBER
There are many Hindu festivals and you are learning about some of the most important ones. You need to know what the festivals celebrate and how people observe these festivals.

Raksha Bandhan – 'knot of protection'

This festival is celebrated just before Janmashtami. Girls tie a thread around their brothers' wrists. The thread is called a rakhi and, in the middle, there is a flower-shaped decoration. The brother gives a present to his sister and promises to protect her for the rest of their lives.

Practice question

■ Do you agree that it is important to celebrate festivals every year?

Practise writing one or two paragraphs in answer to this question. Remember to look at different opinions in your answer. Think carefully about what effect celebrating festivals regularly might have on the life of a Hindu. You might argue that they lose their meaning if you celebrate them too often.

Hindu rites of passage

Birth

The baby is washed and the symbol 'om' is written on his or her tongue with a golden pen. Ten to twelve days after the birth, the priest announces the baby's name and prayers are said. The first time the baby is taken outside the house, the father recites the Gayatri Mantra: *We contemplate the glorious splendour of the divine life-giver; may he enlighten our minds.*

Upanayana – the Sacred Thread ceremony

This ceremony, which is becoming less common, marks the start of the Brahmacharya ashrama (see page 28). It originally marked the stage when a boy left home to live with his guru. When the boy is between eight and sixteen, his head is shaved and he is presented to the household gods. The boy and his father make an offering and recite the Gayatri Mantra. The boy is given the sacred thread – three strings of white cotton of nine strands each, tied with a spiritual knot. This rests from left shoulder to right hip.

Marriage

Weddings take place in the bride's home or the **mandir**. The bride wears a red sari and has mendhi patterns painted on her hands and feet. The groom wears a flower garland and a veil of tassels. The ceremony is conducted by a **brahmin** who recites verses from the Vedas. The couple's hands are tied together by a cord. They take seven steps around the sacred fire – these steps represent food, strength, wealth, fortune, children, seasons and friendship.

Death

A Hindu's funeral should take place within 24 hours of death. The corpse is washed, dressed and taken to the funeral pyre. The eldest son recites prayers from the Vedas and lights the fire. If possible, he takes the ashes to India to scatter them in one of the sacred rivers, in particular, the **Ganga** (Ganges). Today, outside of India, many Hindus are cremated at a crematorium. Hindus believe that death is just part of the journey towards **moksha**.

> **!** **REMEMBER**
> All Hindu rites of passage are closely connected with religion. They mark stages in a Hindu's life from birth to death and then reincarnation.

31

Hinduism

Practice question

■ 'When you are a teenager, you cannot take on adult responsibilities in your religion.' Do you agree?

Practise writing one or two paragraphs in answer to this question. In your answer, you need to be sensitive to what Hindus might think about this issue. Show that you understand different views about what it means to be an adult. Consider whether religious teachings should come first in deciding this.

Hindu pilgrimage

A Hindu pilgrim in the River Ganga

Mother Ganga – the River Ganges

The **Ganga** is the most important place of Hindu pilgrimage. The water is believed to cleanse people from their sins so they can wash away bad **karma**. The Hindu ideal is to be cremated at one of the 'burning ghats' (steps) on the river. When people visit the Ganga, they go into the water and pour some of it over their heads. They stand in the river to pray, make offerings of flowers and fruit and offer the water up to the sun.

Varanasi

The city of Varanasi, sometimes called Benares, is on the Ganga and hundreds of temples line the banks of the river there. It is a very important religious centre.

Mount Kailasha

This mountain is in the centre of the Himalayas and is sacred to Shiva.

Badrinath

Badrinath is also in the Himalayas and has a spring which is part of the source of the Ganga. Many holy men live there.

The temple of Jagannatha

Many followers of Vishnu make a pilgrimage to this temple in Puri for the annual festival there in June or July.

Practice question

■ Choose one place of pilgrimage, explain why it is important for Hindus and the effect which a visit to this place may have when they return home.

Practise writing one or two paragraphs in answer to this question. It is important to answer all parts of the question. Explain why the place you have chosen is important for Hindus and what they might do there. You also need to consider the effect which this visit might have on their everyday life after they return home.

Hindu places of worship

The mandir

In India, there are many ancient **mandirs**, but these vary from small village shrines to very elaborate buildings. Traditional mandirs are surrounded by walls. These walls create space between the temple and the world. There are small shrines inside the walls as well as the temple. The main building has a tall tower which stands over the statue, or **murti**, of the god.

A bell is placed at the entrance to the temple and people ring this as they enter the building. Worshippers also remove their shoes and wash their hands. Inside are the murti of various gods while the principal god of the temple is usually in a shrine at the back.

There is no formal congregational worship in mandirs and no obligation for Hindus to visit them. However, people can visit and make **bhakti** (devotion) at any time. Priests bathe the murtis each day and give them clean clothes. Then the **arti** ceremony takes place in front of the murtis. The **brahmin** has a **puja** tray with a lamp, a fan, a shell, offerings of food, water, flowers, incense and a small bell. Puja is performed while he chants from the scriptures.

The five elements of arti are:
- Fire – the arti lamp (a cotton wick in ghee)
- Earth – flowers and incense
- Water – used to wash the murti
- Air – a fan
- Ether – a conch shell.

The lamp is moved around the murti in a clockwise direction. Both hands are put over the flame with the fingertips touching it. The hands are then moved across the forehead showing that the worshipper is receiving the blessing of God. The arti service ends with everyone sharing prashad – the food which has been offered to the gods. Many Hindus perform this ceremony of puja (worship) each day at the shrines in their homes.

! REMEMBER
A Hindu place of worship in Britain might be very different from one in India. You need to know the most important features which you would probably find in a mandir in any country.

Hinduism

Hindus making bhakti

Practice question

- Explain the meaning and symbolism of the features and furnishings of a mandir.

Practise writing one or two paragraphs in answer to this question. Remember to 'explain the meaning and symbolism' of features and furnishings as well as describing them. You will need to say where they are placed in the building, what they are used for and the Hindu beliefs associated with them.

To answer questions on the following topics, you need to know about:

Islamic beliefs

- what Muslims believe about their God and their religion
- how Muslims show these beliefs in their daily lives.

This section looks at what Muslims believe and why. You will have the opportunity to answer a question about Muslim beliefs and practices.

Islamic holy books

- what the Muslim holy book is and what it contains
- the use which Muslims make of this book in their lives and worship.

This section deals with the Qur'an, what it contains and the way in which Muslims use it today. You will have the opportunity to answer a question about the use which people make of their holy book in their daily lives.

Islamic festivals

- what the main Muslim special times are
- what particular events the special times are celebrating
- how they are celebrated.

This section focuses on the main festivals of Islam. It also gives you the opportunity to practise answering questions about different points of view.

Islamic rites of passage

- the four Muslim rites of passage
- how these are celebrated and why they are important.

You need to remember that not all Muslims celebrate these rites of passage in the same way. You will also have the opportunity to answer a question about rites of passage for which you need to consider different points of view.

Islamic pilgrimage

- Muslim teaching about pilgrimage
- why Muslims go on pilgrimage
- what effect a pilgrimage might have on peoples' lives after they return home.

In this section, you will have the opportunity to answer a question about why people go on pilgrimages and the effect that this might have on them.

Islamic places of worship

- the main features of Muslim places of worship and the reasons for their design
- the principal forms of worship which take place in these buildings.

At the end of this section, you will be given the opportunity to answer a question about the reasons for the design of a mosque.

Islamic beliefs

All religions are about believing in certain things. Islam is about believing in one God, Allah, who guides and protects Muslims in their daily lives.

The obligations for Muslims are that they submit to the will of Allah and follow the teachings of the Qur'an as revealed to the Prophet Muhammad (pbuh).

The Islamic holy books

The Muslim scriptures are called the Qur'an. The Qur'an is the word of Allah as given to Muhammad. It is the final revelation from Allah and is completely divine.

The Qur'an is divided into Surahs (chapters). There are 114 Surahs.

The Surahs are arranged according to length, the longest is first and the shortest is at the end.

All Surahs, except Surah 9, begin with the words 'In the name of Allah, Most Gracious, Most Merciful'.

The Hadith are collections of the practices and sayings of the Prophet. They contain the Sunnah – customs and traditions of Muhammad. The Hadith are treated with great respect, and are next to the Qur'an in importance.

Islamic festivals

The main festivals of the Muslim year are observed with devotion and submission to Allah.

- Ramadan – ninth month of the Muslim year
- Laylat-ul-Qadr – The Night of Power – when Muhammad began to receive the revelation of the Qur'an

- Id-ul-Fitr – celebration of the end of Ramadan and the first day of Shawal
- Id-ul-Adha – celebration of sacrifice at the end of the Hajj
- Mawlid an-Nabi – the birthday of the Prophet
- Muharram – first month of the year – commemorating the Hijrah
- Ashura – 10th Muharram – the day of creation

Islamic rites of passage

The four rites of passage for Muslims are:

- birth – reciting the adhan into the baby's ear
- aqiqa – a ceremony seven days after the birth of a child
- marriage – the blessing of two people who intend to spend the rest of their lives together
- death – the ceremonies when a person dies and hopes to go to heaven.

Pilgrimage

Pilgrimages are not holidays. Muslim pilgrimage is called the Hajj.

Hajj is one of the five pillars of Islam (see page 36).

Giving up time to go on Hajj might help to strengthen a Muslim's faith.

Islamic places of worship

Most Muslims worship both at home and in a mosque.

Mosques are designed to symbolise Muslim beliefs and to help them in their worship.

Mosques are used for the daily prayers.

The most important weekly service is at noon on Friday – Salat-ul-Jumu'ah.

35

Islam

REMEMBER
'Islam' means submission to the will of Allah.

'I believe in Allah, in his angels, in his books, in his messengers, in the Last Day, and in the fact that everything, good or bad is decided by Allah, the almighty, and in life after death'.

The seven basic beliefs of Islam are in three groups:

Tawhid is about the oneness of Allah
- Tawhid (Allah, one God)

Risalah is about prophethood
- Mala'ikha (angels of Allah)
- Kutubullah (books of Allah)
- Rasulullah (messengers of Allah)

Akhirah is about life after death
- Yawmuddin (the Day of Judgement)
- Al-Qadr (predestination)
- Akhirah (life after death)

As part of their submission to the will of Allah, Muslims follow the five pillars which are visible signs of their way of life. The five pillars are:

- **Shahadah** (declaration of faith) – There is no god but Allah; Muhammad is the messenger of Allah
- **Salah** – compulsory prayers five times a day. These are:
  Fajr (between dawn and sunrise)
  Zuhr (after midday)
  Asr (between late afternoon and sunset)
  Maghrib (between sunset and the end of daylight)
  'Isha (night, until dawn)
- **Zakah** – purification of wealth by an annual welfare payment, usually $2^{1}/_{2}\%$ of savings.
- **Hajj** – pilgrimage to Makkah made during the month of Dhul-Hijjah
- **Sawm** – fasting during the hours of daylight at Ramadan.

REMEMBER
When you are answering questions about Islam, you must try to see how a Muslim would feel about a particular idea or situation.

Practice question

- Consider how observing the five pillars might influence the life of a Muslim today.

Practise writing one or two paragraphs in answer to this question. Remember that you need to deal with each of the pillars and explain the effect which observing them might have on a Muslim's life. Make sure that you look at the positive effects of living a religious life as well as any others you may consider.

Islamic holy books

Muslims believe that the **Qur'an** is the final revelation of Allah. The Qur'an mentions three other 'revealed' books:

- Tawrah (the Torah) of Musa (pbuh) (Moses)
- Zabur (the Psalms) of Dawud (pbuh) (David)
- Injil (the Gospel) of 'Isa (pbuh) (Jesus)

Muslims believe that all revealed books, other than the Qur'an, have been changed and corrupted.

 The Qur'an

It is believed that the Qur'an cannot be translated because the original Arabic is the actual word of Allah. The original of the Qur'an is in Heaven. The Qur'an was revealed to **Muhammad** (pbuh) between the years 610-632CE. The first revelation of the Qur'an took place in Ramadan 610CE, in the Cave of Hira, which is on Mount al-Nur. The Angel Jibril (Gabriel) appeared to Muhammad and told him to: *'Proclaim! (or Read!) in the name of thy Lord and Cherisher, Who created – Created man, out of a (mere) clot of congealed blood: Proclaim! And thy Lord is Most Bountiful, – He who taught (the use of) the Pen, – Taught man that which he knew not'.* (Surah 96:1-5)

Muhammad could not read so he learnt the verses and repeated them to others. The revelation ended when the Prophet gave his farewell sermon on ninth Dhul-Hijjah (10 AH).

Before touching or reading the Qur'an, Muslims ensure that they are clean and have performed **wudu** (see page 41). The Qur'an is kept wrapped in a silk cloth on the highest shelf in the house. It is usually placed on a rahal (a low stand or stool) to be read. When reading the Qur'an, a Muslim must avoid talking, eating or drinking. Most Muslims cover their heads while reading.

The Qur'an provides a complete book of guidance for Muslims and covers every aspect of human life. It is also, with the Sunnah (the example of the Prophet), the basis for Shari'ah (the code of living for the Islamic way of life). A person who memorises the Qur'an and can recite it all is called hafiz.

> **REMEMBER**
> As a sign of respect, Muslims say and write 'peace and blessings be upon him' (pbuh) after the name of Muhammad and the other Prophets.

37

Islam

Practice question

■ Explain how Muslims might use the Qur'an to make decisions about how they should live.

Practise writing one or two paragraphs in answer to this question. In your answer, you need to look at the way in which Muslims regard the Qur'an and the great importance they attach to it. You need to look at some of its teachings and then explain how these might influence people's daily lives.

REMEMBER The Muslim year has 354 days instead of the usual 365. This means that there are 33 Muslim years to 32 solar ones. Therefore Islamic festivals are celebrated eleven days earlier each year, according to the Western calendar.

REMEMBER All Muslim festivals are celebrated because they mark important events in the Muslims' religious year and in the life of Muhammad.

Ramadan

Ramadan is one of the five pillars (see page 36). Muslims fast from sunrise to sunset throughout the month to show their devotion and submission to Allah as well as strengthing the ummah, the worldwide community of Muslims.

Laylat-ul-Qadr (the night of power) occurs during the last ten days of Ramadan. It is 'better than a thousand months' (Surah 97:3) because it was when the first revelation of the Qur'an was made.

Id-ul-Fitr, also know as the Lesser Id, marks the end of Ramadan. Prayers are said in the mosque, special meals are eaten and people give charity.

Id-ul-Adha

This festival is also known as the Greater Id and marks the end of the **Hajj**. It celebrates the occasion when Ibrahim was willing to sacrifice his son, Isma'il, for Allah. There are special services in mosques and a goat is sacrificed by each household. The meat is cooked and much of it is given to the poor.

Mawlid an-Nabi

This festival marks the birth and death of the Prophet and falls on the twelfth day of Rabi' ul-Awwal. Many Muslims do not celebrate this festival as Muhammad never celebrated his own birthday.

Muharram

A festival is held on the first day of the first month, Muharram, to commemorate the Hijrah when Muhammad left Makkah for al-Madinah.

Ashura

This is the tenth day of Muharram. It is believed that on this day Allah created the world, Adam was created, Nuh (Noah) left the ark after the flood, Allah saved Musa (Moses) from Pharaoh and the Day of Judgement will take place. Many Muslims mark this day by fasting.

Practice question

■ Do you agree that it is important to celebrate festivals every year?

Practise writing one or two paragraphs in answer to this question. In your answer, look at different opinions. Think carefully about what effect regular celebration of festivals might have on the life of a Muslim. You might argue that they lose their meaning if you celebrate them too often.

Islamic rites of passage

Birth

Muslims consider all newborn babies to be Muslims. The baby's father recites the adhan (the words used during the call to prayer) into the baby's right ear. This is so that the words 'Allah is great' are the first a baby hears.

Aqiqa

This ceremony takes place seven days after birth. The **Imam** (prayer leader) says a prayer in the baby's ear and the baby's head is shaved. The hair is weighed and the equivalent weight of gold or silver is given to charity. Goats or sheep are slaughtered – one for a baby girl; two for a boy. Some boys are circumcised at their aqiqa, but this can be done at any time before they are ten. When children reach puberty, they are answerable for themselves to Allah.

Marriage

A Muslim marriage usually takes place in the home or mosque. The couple give their consent to the marriage before two witnesses. During the ceremony, there are readings from the Qur'an. The Aqd Nikah (contract of marriage) is spoken as well as written. The bride and groom sign three copies of this. The groom gives mahr (a sum of money), some property or another valuable gift to the bride and this remains her property for life.

Death

When Muslims are dying, they say 'Allah, help me through the hardship and agony of death' and also the **Shahadah**. The corpse is washed three times, perfumed and wrapped in a single piece of cloth. The funeral takes place within three days. At the cemetery, prayers and the al-Fatihah (Surah 1) are said. Muslims are buried facing **Makkah**. As they are lowered into the ground, the following is said: *'From the (earth) did We create you, and into it shall We return you, and from it shall We bring you out once again.'* (Surah 20:55).

! REMEMBER
All Muslim rites of passage are associated with prayers and readings from the Qur'an.

39

! REMEMBER
Muslims do not believe in reincarnation.

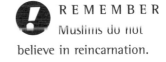

Islam

Practice question

■ 'Religion is a personal thing and people should make decisions for themselves so it is wrong to force a religion onto a baby'. Discuss with special reference to Islam.

Practise writing one or two paragraphs in answer to this question. In your answer, you need to be sensitive to what Muslims might think about this. You need to show that you understand different views about children and religion as well as explaining why it is important for many people that their children should be brought up to be religious from birth.

Islamic pilgrimage

People go on pilgrimage for various reasons:
- because it is one of the five pillars
- to learn more about their religion
- to strengthen their faith
- to feel closer to Allah.

! REMEMBER
Muslims go on Hajj (pilgrimage) because it is one of the five pillars.

Muslim pilgrims at the Ka'bah

📺 Hajj

Hajj is the pilgrimage to **Makkah** made by Muslims during the month of Dhul-Hijjah. (Following the path of the Hajj at a different time of year is called Umrah.) Hajj means 'to set out with a definite purpose'. It is the only one of the five pillars which is not compulsory but every Muslim has the duty to try to make the Hajj if they have enough money to care for any dependants they leave behind (they must not go if it would create hardship for their families.) People who are mentally or physically unfit are also excused from the Hajj.

Pilgrims go on Hajj from 8-13 Dhul-Hijjah. The pilgrimage begins in Makkah. All pilgrims wear the same white clothes – Ihram. This is two pieces of cloth for men and three for women. Ihram shows the equality of all humanity. Men do not shave or cut their hair during the Hajj.

Pilgrims walk around the **Ka'bah** seven times anti-clockwise (tawaf). They walk seven times between the hills of Safa and Marwah (sa'y). This reminds them of the story of Hagar, the wife of Ibrahim, who ran between the two hills looking for water for baby Isma'il. They then travel to the village of Mina where they camp. They go to Arafat before sunrise on the 9th. After sunset, they go to Muzdalifah, where they collect stones. In the morning, they throw these stones at the pillars where Satan tempted Isma'il. At Mina, they sacrifice an animal for **Id-ul-Adha**. The sacrifice reminds them of how Ibrahim was willing to sacrifice his son Isma'il, and of the ram which Allah provided instead. People then shave and return to normal clothes before repeating tawaf. Some pilgrims then go to the tomb of the Prophet at al-Madinah.

For most Muslims, the Hajj is a once-in-a-lifetime event. A man who goes on Hajj is called a Hajji; a woman, a Hajja.

Practice question

- Explain why the Hajj is so important to Muslims and the effect which going on Hajj may have on them when they return home.

Practise writing one or two paragraphs in answer to this question. It is important to answer both parts of the question. You'll need to explain why the Hajj is important for Muslims and what they might do during it. Also consider the effect which this visit might have on their life after they return home.

Islamic places of worship

📺 The mosque

Masjid (mosque) means 'a place of prostration'. The main use of a mosque is as a prayer hall. Mosques are also used for studying, classes and community activities within the ummah.

They are usually built in the form of a square with an open courtyard in the centre. Minarets are at the front or the corners of the mosque. They are a high place from where the adhan (call to prayer) can be made by the mu'adhin (muezzin) as follows:

Allah is the greatest
I bear witness that there is no god but Allah
I bear witness that Muhammad is Allah's messenger
Rush to prayer
Rush to success
Allah is the Greatest
There is no god but Allah
Prayer is better than sleep

Preparing for prayer

The entrance to a mosque has shoe racks so that people can go into the prayer hall barefoot. There are areas for men and women where they can perform **wudu** (the ritual washing) that is required before prayer. Muslims wash their hands, mouth, nostrils, face, arms to the elbow, neck and feet.

The prayer hall is a large open area without seats. Some mosques have Qur'anic inscriptions or mosaic patterns on the walls. The **mihrab** is an alcove in the **Qiblah** wall which shows the direction of Makkah for prayer. The **minbar** is a short flight of stairs with a platform at the top. The **Imam** preaches from this platform at Salat-ul-Jumu'ah (Friday prayers).

There are no statues or pictures of people or animals inside a mosque. A picture or statue of Allah or the Prophets would be idolatry (idol worship). In the prayer hall, there is a separate gallery with a screen for the women so that they cannot distract the men from prayer.

❗ REMEMBER
Mosques are never decorated with pictures of living beings and no one is allowed to attempt to draw a picture of Muhammad or Allah.

Islam

Practice question

■ Explain the meaning and symbolism of the features and furnishings of a mosque.

Practise writing one or two paragraphs in answer to this question. Remember to 'explain the meaning and symbolism' of the features and furnishings as well as describe them. You will need to mention where they are placed in the building, what they are used for and the Muslim beliefs associated with them.

Judaism

To answer questions on the following topics, you need to know about:

Jewish beliefs

- what Jews believe about their God and their religion
- how Jews show these beliefs in their daily lives.

This section focuses on what Jews believe and why. You will have the opportunity to answer a question about particular Jewish beliefs.

Jewish holy books

- what the Jewish holy books are and what they contain
- the use which Jews make of these books in their lives and worship.

This section deals with the Tenakh, what it contains and the way in which Jews use it today. You will have the opportunity to answer a question about the use which people make of their holy books in their daily lives.

Jewish festivals

- what the main Jewish festivals are
- what particular events the festivals are celebrating
- how they are celebrated.

This section focuses on the main festivals of Judaism. It also gives you the opportunity to practise answering questions about different points of view.

Jewish rites of passage

- the four Jewish rites of passage
- how these are celebrated and why they are important.

You need to remember that not all Jews celebrate these rites of passage in the same way. You will also have the opportunity to answer a question about rites of passage for which you need to consider different points of view.

Jewish pilgrimages

- Jewish teaching about pilgrimage
- some places of Jewish pilgrimage
- why Jews might decide to go on a pilgrimage
- what effect a pilgrimage might have on people's lives after they return home.

In this section, you will have the opportunity to answer a question on the reasons people go on pilgrimages and the effects this might have on them.

Jewish places of worship

- the main features of Jewish places of worship and the reasons for their design
- the principal forms of worship which take place in these buildings.

At the end of this section, you will be given the opportunity to answer a question about the reasons for the design of a synagogue.

Jewish beliefs

All religions are about believing in certain things. Judaism is about believing in one God who guides and protects Jews in their daily lives.

The obligations for Jews are that, in the fulfilment of the covenant – the agreement their ancestors made with God – they will worship God and follow his laws.

Jewish holy books

The Jewish scriptures are called the Tenakh. The Tenakh is divided into three sections:

- **The Torah** (Law) contains five books: Genesis, Exodus, Leviticus, Numbers, Deuteronomy.
- **Nevi'im** (Prophets) contains twenty-one books.
- **Ketuvim** (Writings) contains thirteen books.

As well as the Tenakh, or written Torah, there is the Oral Torah, called the Talmud.

Jewish festivals

The main festivals of the Jewish year are either commanded in the Torah or celebrate historical events:

- Shabbat – the Sabbath
- The three pilgrim festivals (before the destruction of the Temple in 70CE, Jews made a pilgrimage to Jerusalem to make offerings of the harvest at these times):
  Pesach (Passover) – celebrates the Exodus from Egypt
  Shavuot – Feast of Weeks
  Sukkot – Feast of Tabernacles
- Simchat Torah
- The Yom Tovim:
  Rosh Hashanah – New Year
  Yom Kippur – Day of Atonement

- Historical festivals:
  Purim – Feast of Lots
  Hanukkah

All Jewish festivals begin and end at sunset.

Jewish rites of passage

The four rites of passage for Jews are:

- brit milah – circumcision of boys when they are eight days old
- bar mitzvah or bat mitzvah – a ceremony marking the beginning of adult life
- marriage – the blessing of two people who intend to spend the rest of their lives together
- death – the ceremonies when a person dies and hopes to go to heaven.

Jewish pilgrimages

Pilgrimages are not holidays. The original Jewish pilgrimages were to Jerusalem to celebrate the pilgrim festivals.

Since the destruction of the Temple, there are no actual Jewish pilgrimages.

Most places that Jews visit on pilgrimage are in Israel.

Giving up time to go on a pilgrimage might help to strengthen Jews' faith, help them feel closer to God or learn more about their religion.

Jewish places of worship

The home is the main focus for Jewish life and worship. Community worship takes place in a synagogue.

The different designs of buildings used for worship often reflect the beliefs and views of a particular group. Synagogues are designed to symbolise the beliefs of Jews and to help them in their worship.

43

REMEMBER
When answering questions about Jewish beliefs, it is important to make clear that Jews are monotheists – that is, they believe that there is only one God.

Nearly 4000 years ago in Mesopotamia, the prophet Abraham was told by God to leave his home in the city of Ur. He was told to worship one God and made an agreement to do this in about 1900BCE. In return, God promised to look after Abraham and his descendants and lead them to the Promised Land of Canaan. Later, after many years of suffering in Egypt, the Jews were led back to the Promised Land by Moses who made a new covenant with God. In Exodus 19:5-6, God promises that the obedience of the Jews will make them a holy nation belonging to Him.

At this time, God gave the Jews the Ten Commandments:
- You shall worship no other gods besides me.
- Do not worship idols.
- Do not take God's name in vain.
- Observe the Sabbath and keep it holy.
- Honour your father and mother.
- Do not kill.
- Do not commit adultery.
- Do not steal.
- Do not tell lies.
- Do not envy other people's property.

These Commandments provide the basic rules of Jewish life.

The central statement of Jewish belief is found in a prayer called the **Shema**. This is a collection of several verses from the **Tenakh**:

Hear, O Israel: The Lord our God; the Lord is one. And thou shalt love the Lord thy God with all thy heart, and with all thy soul, and with all thy might. And these words, which I command thee this day, shall be in thy heart: and thou shalt teach them diligently to thy children, and shalt talk of them when thou sittest in thy house, and when thou walkest by the way, and when thou liest down, and when thou risest up. And thou shalt bind them as a sign upon thy arm, and they shall be as frontlets between thy eyes. And thou shalt write them upon the doorposts of thy house, and on thy gates. (Deuteronomy 6:4-9)

The Shema is said several times a day. Saying the Shema and keeping the Ten Commandments are constant reminders to Jews throughout their daily lives.

Practice question

- Explain why the Shema and the Ten Commandments are still so important to Jews today.

Practise writing one or two paragraphs in answer to this question. Remember to write about both the Ten Commandments and the Shema. You need to consider why these are important as well as the effect which they might have on the life of a Jew.

Jewish holy books

📺 The Torah

The books of the **Torah** – the source of Jewish teachings, practices and customs – are written in a **Sefer Torah** or scroll. The parchment scroll contains the Hebrew text, handwritten by a scribe with a goose feather.

The Torah scrolls are treated with great respect in the **synagogue** where they are kept in the ark (see page 49). The scrolls are covered with elaborate mantles. Over these is a silver breastplate and a yad. A **yad** is a pointer in the shape of an arm and hand. It is used to ensure that the person reading the scroll does not come into contact with the text.

The scroll is carried around the synagogue in procession, then taken to the **bimah** (reading desk). The scroll is held up and turned to all sides so that everyone can see it. Parts of the Torah are read during services on Sabbaths, festivals, new moons, fast days and every Monday and Thursday. After the Torah reading is the Haftavah, a reading from the Nevi'im and Ketuvim.

The whole Torah is read during the year. The final reading takes place on **Simchat Torah** (Rejoicing in the Torah) when the final words of the book of Deuteronomy are read in the same breath as the first words of the book of Genesis so that the cycle starts once more (see page 46).

The Torah is believed to be the revealed word of God, given directly to Moses who wrote it down. Therefore nothing in the written Torah can be changed. History says that the oral Torah was given to Moses at the same time as he wrote down the written Torah. The oral Torah guides Jews on how, and when, to observe the 613 mitzvot (commandments) found in the written Torah. The oral Torah, know as the **Talmud**, contains two parts:

- the **Mishnah**, which was put together by Rabbi Judah the Prince in c.200CE and has sixty-three volumes including Halakhah and Hagadah
- the **Gemara**, the comments of later rabbis.

The Talmud also has a very important part to play in Jewish life and many of the rules and practices of daily life are found there.

❗ REMEMBER
The Torah scrolls are believed to contain the actual words of God given to Moses, and they are shown great respect.

45

Practice question

- Explain how Jews might use the written Torah and the oral Torah to make decisions about how they should live.

Practise writing one or two paragraphs in answer to this question. Notice that you are asked to write about both the written Torah and the oral Torah. You must do this in order to achieve good marks. You need to explain the differences between them and the importance which Jews give to them. You then need to explain how teachings from both might influence people's daily lives.

Jewish festivals

46

Shabbat

Shabbat (the Sabbath) is celebrated every week. As one of the Ten Commandments, Jews must rest from work from Friday evening to Saturday evening. Friday evening is a special time in a Jewish home with the family eating and praying together. Services are held in the synagogue. The Sabbath ends with the ceremony of **Havdalah** (separation).

REMEMBER Most Jewish festivals are celebrated because there are instructions about them in the Torah.

Pilgrim festivals

Pesach (Passover): 15-20 Nisan. During this time, Jews have special **Seder** meals in which the story of the Exodus is retold and symbolic foods are eaten. No yeast is allowed in Jewish homes during this time.

Shavuot: 6-7 Sivan. This festival remembers the wheat harvest and the giving of the Torah to Moses.

Sukkot (Tabernacles): 15-22 Tishri. Jews build a hut or **Sukkah** in their gardens and eat there to remember how their ancestors lived in the desert.

Simchat Torah

This takes place on 23 Tishri and celebrates the Torah. The scrolls are carried around the synagogue by people dancing and singing.

REMEMBER Not all Jewish festivals are times of celebration. High holy days, such as Yom Kippur, are times of serious reflection.

The Yom Tovim

Rosh Hashanah (New Year): 1-2 Tishri. There are services in the synagogue and people eat apples and honey so that the New Year will be sweet.

Yom Kippur (Day of Atonement): 10 Tishri. With fasting and worship, Jews ask God to forgive the Jewish community for the sins of the past year.

Historical festivals

Purim (the Feast of Lots): 14 Adar. The story of Esther is celebrated with a service in the synagogue and with parties.

Hanukkah: celebrated for eight days beginning on 25 Kislev. It recalls the victory of the Maccabees in taking the Temple back from the Greeks.

Practice question

■ Do you agree that it is important to celebrate festivals every year?

Practise writing one or two paragraphs in answer to this question. Remember to look at different opinions in your answer. Think about what effect celebrating festivals regularly might have on the life of a Jew. You might argue that they lose their meaning if you celebrate them too often.

BITESIZEreligious education

Jewish rites of passage

Brit milah

Babies are taken to the synagogue on the **Shabbat** after their birth and welcomed into the congregation by their Hebrew name. When a baby boy is eight days old, he is **circumcised** because God said to Abraham: '*This is my covenant, which you shall keep, between me and you and thy seed after thee; Every man-child among you shall be circumcised*'. (Genesis 17:10). The baby's foreskin is removed by a trained man called a **mohel**. Prayers are said and the baby is given a drop of wine.

! REMEMBER
All Jewish boys must be circumcised as part of the covenant God made with the Jews.

47

Bar and bat mitzvah

Boys are considered adults when they are thirteen, and girls when they are twelve. They are then responsible for their own faith. **Bar mitzvah** means 'son of the commandment'. **Bat mitzvah** means 'daughter of the commandment' (although this ceremony is not recognised by many Orthodox Jews). At his bar mitzvah, the boy reads a passage from the Torah. There is usually a party after the service. The son thanks his father and the father thanks God that he is no longer responsible for his son's religious upbringing.

Jewish girl at her bat mitzvah

Marriage

At a Jewish wedding, a **huppah** (canopy) is held over the couple to represent their new home together. They make a statement of legal responsibility, then the groom gives the bride a ring. Prayers are said, the **ketubah** (marriage contract) is read and the Sheva Berachot (seven blessings) are sung. At the end of the ceremony, the groom smashes a glass with his foot and everyone shouts 'Mazel Tov!' (good luck).

Death

When a Jewish person is known to be dying, he or she tries to say the **Shema** (see page 44). The Hevra Kaddisha (Holy Society or Burial Committee) prepare the corpse and arrange the funeral, which should take place within 24 hours.

! REMEMBER
If you are discussing Jewish beliefs about death, remember that Jews do not believe in reincarnation.

Practice question

■ 'When you are a teenager, you cannot be an adult in your religion.' Do you agree?

Practise writing one or two paragraphs in answer to this question. In your answer, you need to be sensitive to what Jews might think about this issue. You need to show that you understand different views about what it means to be an adult and whether religious teachings should come first in making this sort of decision.

Jewish pilgrimage

Although Jews no longer have to go on pilgrimage as part of their religion, there are many places which attract pilgrims.

A Jew praying at the Western Wall

Jerusalem

After the Temple was destroyed in 70CE, the festivals once celebrated in Jerusalem were celebrated in the home and synagogue (see page 46). The Jews were driven out of Israel many times; finally, by the Romans in 70CE. The State of Israel was established in 1948, and since then, many Jews have returned. The Temple Mount in Jerusalem (Mount Moriah) is the site of the original Temple. The Western Wall was part of the wall built by Herod to surround the Temple. Many boys celebrate their **bar mitzvah** here. Many Jews pray at the Wall and put prayers on folded pieces of paper in its cracks.

Masada

Masada is a mountain near the Dead Sea. In 74CE, one thousand Jewish men, women and children committed suicide here rather than accept Roman rule.

Yad Vashem

Yad Vashem means 'a place and a name' and it commemorates the **Shoah** (Holocaust) of World War II when over six million Jews were killed by the Nazis. It contains the 'Avenue of the Righteous Gentiles' which remembers non-Jews who risked their lives to save Jewish people. In the Hall of Remembrance, the names of the 22 concentration camps can be seen and an eternal light marks the place where ashes from various crematoria are buried.

Auschwitz

Two million people were murdered by the Nazis at Auschwitz concentration camp in Poland during World War II. Millions of pilgrims visit the Auschwitz-Birkenau Museum every year to remember the victims.

> ❗ **REMEMBER** Since the destruction of the Temple in 70CE, Jews have not been able to go there for the Pilgrim Festivals.

Practice question

■ Choose one place of pilgrimage, explain why it is important for Jews and how a visit to this place may help them when they return home.

Practise writing one or two paragraphs in answer to this question. It is important to answer all parts of the question. You will need to explain why the place you have chosen is important for Jews and what they might do there. Also consider the effect which this visit might have on their everyday life after they return home.

Jewish places of worship

The synagogue

The word 'synagogue' is Greek for 'bringing together'. The Hebrew names for a synagogue include **Bet ha knesset** ('house of assembly') and Bet ha midrash ('house of learning'). Most Jews use the name Shul (Yiddish for 'school'). Synagogues are very plain on the outside. They are usually rectangular. Inside a synagogue, there are no pictures but there may be texts from the Torah used as decoration. Jewish symbols may be placed around the ark. These include the two tablets of stone given to Moses, crowns, the star of David, the lions of Judah and **menorah** (seven-branched candlesticks).

The **Aron Hakodesh** (ark) is the most important feature of every synagogue as the **Sefer Torah** are kept in it. The ark is on the east wall of the synagogue facing Jerusalem. The **Ner Tamid** (eternal light) hangs above the ark to show that God is always present. The **bimah** is a platform and reading desk in front of the ark. Seating is arranged around the bimah so that everyone can see the ark. In Orthodox synagogues, men and women sit separately. The women sit in a gallery or behind a screen. This is so that they do not distract the men. In Progressive synagogues, men and women sit together.

Use of the synagogue

Bet tefillah – house of prayer.
Bet ha midrash – house of study – there are regular classes for children, and often for adults as well.
Bet ha knesset – house of assembly – a regular meeting place.
Bet ha'am – house of people – services of worship are held for all Jews here.

Men and married women cover their heads before entering the synagogue and men wear a tallit (prayer shawl) for morning prayer. In an Orthodox synagogue, services are almost entirely in Hebrew. Prayers are led by the chazan who chants the words. The most important part of a service is when the Sefer Torah is carried to the bimah and read. There must be a **minyan** (at least ten men) in the synagogue for the service to take place. In Progressive synagogues, services take place partly in Hebrew and partly in English. Services are shorter but the central point is still the reading of the Torah.

> **! REMEMBER**
> Synagogues are very plain buildings. They are never decorated with pictures of living beings and no one is allowed to attempt to draw a picture of God.

49

Practice question

■ Explain the meaning and symbolism of the features and furnishings of a synagogue.

Practise writing one or two paragraphs in answer to this question. Remember to 'explain the meaning and symbolism' of the features and furnishings as well as describe them. You will need to say where they are placed in the building, what they are used for and the Jewish beliefs associated with them.

To answer questions on the following topics, you need to know about:

Sikh beliefs

- what Sikhs believe about their God, Waheguru, and their religion
- how Sikhs show these beliefs in their daily lives.

This section focuses on what Sikhs believe and why. You will have the opportunity to answer a question about particular Sikh beliefs.

Sikh holy books

- what the Sikh holy book is and what it contains
- the use which Sikhs make of this book in their lives and worship.

You will have the opportunity to answer a question about the use which people make of their holy books in their daily lives.

Sikh festivals

- what the main Sikh festivals are
- what particular events the festivals are celebrating
- how they are celebrated.

This section focuses on the main festivals of Sikhism. It also gives you the opportunity to practise answering questions about different points of view.

Sikh rites of passage

- the four Sikh rites of passage
- how these are celebrated and why they are important.

You need to remember that not all Sikhs celebrate these rites of passage in the same way. You will also have the opportunity to answer a question about rites of passage for which you need to consider different points of view.

Sikh pilgrimage

- Sikh teaching about pilgrimage
- some places which Sikhs might visit
- why Sikhs might decide to make this sort of trip
- what effect a visit such as this might have on people's lives after they return home.

In this section, you will have the opportunity to answer a question on the reasons people go on religious visits and the effects this might have on them.

Sikh places of worship

- how Sikh traditions have influenced the buildings they use for worship
- the main features of Sikh places of worship and the reasons for their design
- the principal forms of worship which take place in these buildings.

At the end of this section, you will be given the opportunity to answer a question about the reasons for the design of a gurdwara.

Sikh beliefs

All religions are about believing in certain things. Sikhism is about believing in one God who guides and protects Sikhs in their daily lives.

God created the world for people to use and enjoy.

God is present in every soul but is only seen by those he blesses.

Sikhs follow the teachings of the ten Gurus and the Guru Granth Sahib Ji (Sikh scriptures). The ten gurus are:

Guru Nanak Dev Ji: founder of Sikhism
Guru Angad Dev Ji: collected Guru Nanak's hymns together
Guru Amar Das Ji: encouraged the use of the langar (see page 57)
Guru Ram Das Ji: founded the city of Amritsar
Guru Arjan Dev Ji: built the Golden Temple and compiled the Adi Granth
Guru Har Gobind Ji: built the Akal Takht, the political meeting place at Amritsar, and created the Sikh flag, the Nishan Sahib
Guru Har Rai Ji: said that no Sikh could change the Hymns of the Gurus because they are the words of God
Guru Har Krishan Ji: died aged eight
Guru Tegh Bahadur Ji: died protecting both Sikhs and Hindus
Guru Gobind Singh Ji: founded the Khalsa (see page 55) and named the Guru Granth Sahib Ji as his successor.

Sikh holy books

The Sikh scriptures are called the Guru Granth Sahib Ji.

They are written in Punjabi using the Gurmukhi script.

The Guru Granth Sahib Ji is a collection of the teachings and writings of Guru Nanak Dev Ji and five other Gurus.

The Guru Granth Sahib is treated as a true and living Guru.

Sikh festivals

There are two main types of festival in Sikhism:

- gurpurbs – anniversaries of the Gurus
- melas – celebrations held on the same days as Hindu festivals, but which have special meanings for Sikhs and the anniversaries of great events in Sikh history.

Sikh rites of passage

The four rites of passage for Sikhs are:

- birth and naming ceremonies
- Amrit Sanskar – joining the Khalsa. The Khalsa was instituted by Guru Gobind Singh Ji on Baisakhi, 1699
- Anand Karaj (marriage) – the blessing of two people who intend to spend the rest of their lives together
- death – the ceremonies when a person dies.

Sikh pilgrimage

Sikhs do not make pilgrimages.

Visits to holy places are called yatras.

Sikhs might visit Amritsar or Anandpur Sahib.

Giving up time to go on a yatra might help to strengthen a Sikh's faith.

Sikh places of worship

Most Sikhs worship in a gurdwara (see page 57).

Gurdwaras are designed to symbolise the beliefs of Sikhs and to help them in their worship.

📺 Sikh beliefs

The Mool Mantar

The **Mool Mantar** is the most basic statement of Sikh belief and is the first part of morning prayer.

There is only one God
Eternal truth is His name
He is the creator
He is without fear
He is without hate
Immortal, without form
Beyond birth and death
He is the enlightener
He can be reached through the mercy and grace of the true Guru.

❗ REMEMBER It is important to recognise that Sikhs believe that they must live their life so that, at last, they can be liberated from the cycle of rebirth and reach union with God.

Belief in karma and rebirth

Sikhs believe that all actions have consequences so a person's life now is the result of how they lived in a previous life. In each life, a person should try to be better and so come closer to God. Being born a Sikh is, in itself, the result of good **karma**, because the person now has the best chance of hearing God's word and being liberated from the cycle of rebirth to reach union with God. A Sikh 'disciple' is a person who follows the teachings of the ten Gurus (see page 51) and the Guru Granth Sahib Ji (the eternal Guru – see page 53).

Sikh conduct

Sikhs believe they should work hard, share with others and lead a truthful life. They should live a married life that is humble and simple, avoiding lust, anger, greed, arrogance and attachment to worldly things.

Sikhs believe that the whole human race is one and distinctions of caste, colour and class are wrong. Men and women, also, are equal in God's eyes. Sikhs should dress simply and modestly. Sikh women should not wear a veil; neither should anyone make holes in their ears and noses. Idols, magic, omens, fasts and sacred threads are banned. Sikhs should put their faith in the Guru Granth Sahib Ji alone.

Practice question

■ Explain why the lives and teachings of the Gurus are still so important to Sikhs today.

Practise writing one or two paragraphs in answer to this question. Remember to write about more than one of the Gurus. You need to consider why their lives and teachings are important, as well as the effect which they might have on the life of a Sikh.

Sikh holy books

The Guru Granth Sahib Ji

The oldest writings in the Guru Granth Sahib Ji are those of Guru Nanak Dev Ji, the founder of Sikhism. These were written down by Guru Angad Dev Ji. Guru Amar Das Ji and Guru Ram Das Ji both added more hymns. The Adi Granth was put together by Guru Arjan Dev Ji. Guru Gobind Singh Ji added hymns written by Guru Tegh Bahadur Ji and said that after his death, the Guru Granth Sahib Ji should be treated as a living guru.

Every copy of the Guru Granth Sahib Ji is identical, with 1430 pages. Translations are not used. It is written in Punjabi, using Gurmukhi (meaning 'from the mouth of the Guru') script. It is impossible to over-emphasise the importance of the Guru Granth Sahib Ji for Sikhs, who believe that the bani (message within the Guru Granth Sahib Ji) is literally the word of God.

Respect for the Guru Granth Sahib Ji

In every **gurdwara**, there is a resting place containing a bed. Each night, the Guru Granth Sahib Ji is taken there and put to bed. At the beginning of each day, the **granthi** (reader of the Guru Granth Sahib Ji), and any other people present, carry the Guru Granth Sahib Ji in procession to its position in the prayer hall of the gurdwara. It is placed on a cushion in the **manji** – a raised platform covered with a canopy and decorated with flowers and lights. When not in use, the book is covered with a cloth called a romolla. The Guru Granth Sahib Ji is never placed on the ground and no one turns their back to it.

When they enter a gurdwara, Sikhs approach the manji and kneel with their foreheads touching the floor to show respect. The reader or granthi can be anyone who is a member of the **Khalsa** (see page 55). During the readings, the pages are fanned with a **chauri** made of yak's hair. The Guru Granth Sahib Ji is read completely after funerals and during **gurpurbs** (see page 54) – this reading is called the **akhand path**.

Sikh families may have a copy of the Dasam Granth in their home. This is poetry written by Guru Gobind Singh Ji which is not included in the Guru Granth Sahib Ji. They may also have a prayer book called the Nit Nem.

! REMEMBER The Guru Granth Sahib Ji is always treated as a living person.

Practice question

■ Explain how Sikhs might use the Guru Granth Sahib Ji to make decisions about how they should live.

Practise writing one or two paragraphs in answer to this question. You need to explain the origin and contents of the Guru Granth Sahib Ji as well as the importance which Sikhs attach to it. You then need to explain how teachings from it might influence people's daily lives.

Sikh festivals

REMEMBER
All Sikh festivals celebrate important events in Sikh history or in the lives of the Gurus.

54

Gurpurbs

The most important **gurpurbs** are:

- the martyrdom of Guru Arjan Dev Ji (May/June)
- the installation of the Guru Granth Sahib Ji (August/early September)
- the birthday of Guru Nanak Dev Ji (November)
- the birthday of Guru Gobind Singh Dev Ji (December)
- the martyrdom of Guru Tegh Bahadur Dev Ji (December).

At a gurpurb, the Guru Granth Sahib Ji is read from beginning to end – the **akhand path**. On the last day of the reading, Sikhs go to the **gurdwara** to listen. In India, gurpurbs are celebrated on the day of the event, but in countries with small Sikh communities, they are held on the nearest Sunday.

Melas

Baisakhi

Baisakhi falls on 13 April (14 April once every 36 years) and celebrates the Sikh New Year. The **Nishan Sahib** (Sikh flag) is washed. The akhand path is read and initiation ceremonies take place. Originally a Hindu festival celebrating the wheat harvest, Guru Gobind Singh Ji gave a new meaning to Baisakhi in 1699, when he gathered Sikhs from all over the Punjab and formed the first **Khalsa** (the community of the pure). Sikhs also remember the massacre of 400 Sikhs by British soldiers in 1919 at Jallianwala Bagh.

Diwali Mela

Diwali is a Hindu festival in the autumn which marks the end of the rainy season. For Sikhs, it recalls how Guru Har Gobind Ji was released from prison taking fifty-two Hindu prisoners with him. At Diwali, homes and businesses are decorated with divas (clay lamps), candles and coloured lights. There are special family meals and fireworks.

Hola Mohalla Mela

This festival was established by Guru Gobind Singh Ji in 1700 with a three day event of military manoeuvres. At Anandpur, Sikhs celebrate the festival with a fair, including singing, poetry, discussions and physical competitions.

REMEMBER
When you are writing about Sikhism, you must try to see how a Sikh would feel about a particular idea or situation.

Practice question

- Do you agree that it is important to celebrate festivals every year?

Practise writing one or two paragraphs in answer to this question. In your answer, you need to look at different opinions. You should also think carefully about what effect celebrating festivals regularly might have on the life of a Sikh. You might argue that they lose their meaning if you celebrate them too often.

Sikh rites of passage

Birth and name-giving

When a baby is born, the words of the **Mool Mantar** (see page 52) are whispered into its ear and a drop of honey placed on its tongue. At a special ceremony at the gurdwara, the name of the baby is chosen by opening the Guru Granth Sahib Ji at random – the name must begin with the first letter of the hymn on the left hand side of the page. **Singh** ('lion') is added if the baby is a boy, and **Kaur** ('princess') if it is a girl.

Joining the Khalsa – Amrit Sanskar

If they accept the principles of Sikhism, people are able to join the Khalsa when they are fourteen to sixteen years old. Khalsa Sikhs observe the **panj kakke** – the Five Ks. These are:

- **kesh** (uncut hair)
- **kangha** (wooden comb)
- **kachera** (short trousers)
- **kirpan** (short sword)
- **kara** (iron or steel bangle).

Amrit (made from sugar and water) is prepared in an iron bowl. It is blessed and stirred with a khanda (double-edged sword). The amrit is sprinkled on the hair and eyes, the Mool Mantar is recited and **karah parshad** is distributed.

Sikhs wearing some of the five Ks

Anand karaj – marriage

A Sikh wedding is preceded by a betrothal ceremony when verses from the Guru Granth Sahib Ji are read. The wedding takes place in a gurdwara. The bride wears red and gold and covers her head with a red chunni (scarf). The groom carries a long kirpan. The lavan (wedding hymn) of Guru Ram Das Ji is sung and the couple walk four times around the Guru Granth Sahib Ji.

Death

Sikhs believe in reincarnation. When a Sikh is dying, close relatives will say sukhmani (hymn of peace). The corpse is taken to the gurdwara in a coffin. Then it goes to the cremation ground where it is cremated on a funeral pyre.

Practice question

- 'You cannot be an adult in your religion when you are a teenager.' Do you agree?

Practise writing one or two paragraphs in answer to this question. In your answer, you need to be sensitive to what Sikhs might think about this issue. You need to show that you understand different views about what it means to be an adult and whether religious teachings should come first in making this sort of decision.

Sikh pilgrimage

! REMEMBER
It is important to say in any answer on Sikh pilgrimage that Sikhs believe that everywhere is holy because God is everywhere.

56

Sikhs believe that God is everywhere and therefore no place is more holy than any other, and there are no places of Sikh pilgrimage. Sikhs may, however, make visits, called yatras, to places associated with the Gurus or with other important events in Sikh history.

Harmandir Sahib – the Golden Temple at Amritsar

The Golden Temple at Amritsar is a very special gurdwara. The site was chosen by Guru Nanak Dev Ji and Guru Ram Das Ji built a large rectangular pool there, filled with **amrit**. Guru Arjan Dev Ji built the Harmandir on an island in the middle of the pool. The Harmandir has often been at the centre of instances of Sikh persecution. The upper half of the building and the dome is covered in gold leaf. There is a door in each wall to show that everyone is equal. Anyone who visits the Harmandir is welcome to eat at the langar (see page 57) there.

Akal Takht – throne of the divine

This was built by Guru Har Gobind Ji and faces the Harmandir. The Guru Granth Sahib Ji of the Harmandir is kept here. The building is also used as the Sikh high court. Outside are two flag poles, one has the flag of miri (temporal authority) and the other piri (spiritual authority).

Anandpur Sahib

Anandpur Sahib is a very special place for Sikhs. It is in a valley at the foot of the Himalayas. Guru Gobind Singh Ji founded the **Khalsa** here and it is the centre of celebrations for Hola Mohalla Mela (see page 54).

Practice question

■ Choose one place of Sikh yatra, explain why it is important for Sikhs and the effect which a visit to this place may have when they return home.

Practise writing one or two paragraphs in answer to this question. It is important to answer all parts of the question. You need to explain why the place you have chosen is important for Sikhs and what they might do there. You also need to consider the effect which this visit might have on their everyday life after they return home.

Sikh places of worship

The gurdwara

Gurdwara means 'door of the Guru'. A gurdwara is any building in which the **Guru Granth Sahib Ji** can be kept, where Sikhs worship together and where they can eat together in the **langar** – the Guru's kitchen.

Outside the gurdwara is a flag pole. The Sikh flag or **Nishan Sahib** is orange. It has the Khanda on it: two curved kirpans (swords), a khanda (double-edged sword) and a chakkar (circle). At the entrance to the gurdwara is a shoe rack, as shoes cannot be worn in the prayer hall. There are also taps for washing before worship and spare head coverings.

The main prayer hall is a large carpeted area. The sadhsangat (congregation) sit on the floor cross-legged, men and women separately. At one end is the **manji** (a raised platform) with a **chanani** (canopy), where the Guru Granth Sahib Ji is placed. The gurdwara has a rest room with a bed and a canopy for the Guru Granth Sahib Ji to rest at night.

The other main feature is the langar. Everyone eats together in the langar after the services. This shows the Sikh belief in equality and sewa (service to others). All food is vegetarian so that it can be eaten by anyone from any religion.

Worship in the gurdwara

Most Sikh services take place on a Sunday as this is the most convenient day. After bowing to the Guru Granth Sahib Ji, people sit on the floor. The service consists of people chanting verses from the Guru Granth Sahib Ji with **ragis** (musicians) singing and providing accompaniment on musical instruments. A sermon is given based on an explanation of the readings from the Guru Granth Sahib Ji. At the end of the service, a series of prayers from the Gurus is made. While the **ardas** (prayers) are being said, a member of the congregation prepares the **karah parshad** (a sweet offering that is shared amongst everyone) by stirring it with a **kirpan** (ceremonial knife). After the service, the congregation eat a langar (communal meal).

Sharing karah parshad at the gurdwara

> **!** REMEMBER
> The two most important things about a gurdwara are that there is a copy of the Guru Granth Sahib Ji and also a langar.

Practice question

- Explain the meaning and symbolism of the features and furnishings of a gurdwara.

Practise writing one or two paragraphs in answer to this question. Remember to 'explain the meaning and symbolism' of the features and furnishings, not just describe them. Talk about where they are placed in the building, what they are used for and the Sikh beliefs associated with them.

Life after death

To answer questions on this topic, you need to know about:

- how members of the religion you are studying understand the idea of the 'soul', 'spirit' or 'atman'. Be careful if you are studying Buddhism as Buddhists believe that people do not have any kind of everlasting soul
- what happens during a funeral and the reasons for these customs
- what the religion you are studying says about life after death, whether there are beliefs in heaven, hell, and purgatory, or whether there is a belief in rebirth. You need to be able to describe and explain these beliefs
- how these different beliefs affect behaviour – for example, if you believe that there is a God who will judge you when you die, then you are likely to try to find out how God wants you to behave and to put it into practice. If you believe that your actions 'bear fruit' (karma) and that your next life will be more comfortable if you behave well in this life, then this will affect the things you do and the decisions you make.

This section focuses on two aspects of religion:

- beliefs about life after death
- the ways in which these different beliefs are reflected in different funeral customs.

It also gives you practice in answering questions which require one or two paragraphs. You need to be able to explain, in detail, the customs of the religion you are studying. You also need to show that you understand why these customs are important by giving the reasons for them as well as a description.

You need to know the following key points:

- Religious believers do not think that death is the end. They believe that life goes on, in a different way, once a person's body has died.

- Belief that a person is reborn into this world is called reincarnation, rebirth or rebecoming. Hindus, Buddhists and Sikhs share this belief.

- Belief that a person's soul lives on in a new kind of life to be judged by God is shared by Christians, Muslims and many Jews.

- Different religions have different funeral customs which illustrate their beliefs about life after death.

- Funerals include many symbolic objects and actions which remind people of religious teaching. The funeral also gives relatives time to grieve for the people they have lost and provides comfort to mourners.

- Most religions, except for Buddhism, believe that each person has a soul or a Self, which is immortal (does not die). Although the body dies, the soul or Self lives on.

- For Hindus and Sikhs, the soul lives on by being reborn into this world in a new body. Christians, Muslims and many Jews believe that the soul escapes from the body and starts a new kind of existence – for example, in heaven.

- Religious believers think that the way people behave in this life will affect what happens to them after death. Their moral behaviour (whether they choose right or wrong) is rewarded or punished. In Judaism, Christianity and Islam, the reward is everlasting life in heaven. In Hinduism, Buddhism and Sikhism, a person who has lived a good life will be reborn into a better new life because of the workings of karma.

59

Life after death

Beyond the grave

60

Jewish beliefs

Jews believe that people have immortal (living forever) souls, but they do not try to say what life after death will be like. Some Jews believe that a Messiah will come one day and raise the dead on the Day of Judgement. Jews believe that everyone will be judged by God. People will get what they deserve because God does not make mistakes. Jews therefore try to live in a way which will please God, by following the rules set down in the **Torah**.

A Jewish funeral is arranged promptly and simply. The coffin is plain and the funeral service is simple. Many male Jews are buried in their prayer shawls, but without the fringes, to show that they no longer need to keep the laws. Orthodox Jews do not allow cremation. A time for mourning is important for friends and relatives. They sit on low stools and other people look after them while they think about the dead person and try to come to terms with their loss (see page 47 for more about Jewish beliefs).

A Jewish graveyard

Christian beliefs

Christians believe that each person has a soul and that people only live one life. They believe that the death of Jesus, and his **resurrection**, means that God has forgiven them for their **sins** and that they can be confident of a place in heaven. Roman Catholics believe that only those who have led a very pure life will go to be with God immediately. Others will spend some time in **purgatory**, where their own prayers and the prayers of those still living, will take their sins away so that they can enter heaven. Some Christians believe in **hell** – the state of being in which people who have turned their backs on God are separated from God forever.

Christians can be either buried or cremated. A Christian funeral service focuses on the hope of being raised from the dead (see page 23 for more about Christian beliefs).

Muslim beliefs

Muslims believe that we only live one life, which is a preparation for life after death. They believe that everyone will be judged by Allah according to how well they have pleased him and followed his teaching. They try during their lives to please Allah by following the teachings of the Qur'an and living according to the five pillars (see page 36 for more about Muslim beliefs).

Muslims believe that when people die, they should be buried (not cremated) quickly and with a simple ceremony. Rich and poor people should be treated equally. When the dead are in their graves, they will be questioned by **angels**. This decides whether they will wait in comfort or in pain for the Last Day. The Last Day is the end of all life on Earth. The living will be judged by Allah, and the dead will also be brought back to life for judgement.

Consider the ways in which different beliefs about life after death are reflected in different funeral customs.

REMEMBER
Exam questions usually ask you to apply your knowledge. In other words, you should show that you understand that belonging to a religion has an effect on the way people behave and think.

Practice questions

■ How might belief in the Day of Judgement affect a Muslim's behaviour towards other people?

Practise writing one or two paragraphs about how beliefs about life after death in the religion that you are studying might affect a believer's behaviour.

For this question, you need to say what Muslims believe about the Day of Judgement in one or two sentences, but most of your answer should concentrate on how this affects their treatment of other people. You might say that Muslims would give money to charity, that they would look after the elderly, be faithful to their husbands or wives, work against racism and so on, because they want to be judged as good and faithful Muslims. A good answer will give lots of different examples.

■ 'The present day is much more important than life after death.' Do you agree? Give reasons to support your answer, and show that you have thought about different points of view. You must refer to Christianity in your answer.

Practise writing one or two paragraphs in answer to this question, referring to the religion you are studying.

For this question, try and explain how a Christian might answer this, and then give your own view, always giving a reason: 'A Christian might say ... because ...' or 'My view is.... because...'

Death and rebirth

Hindu beliefs

Hindus believe that everyone has an eternal soul, called **atman**, which dies and is reborn many times. They believe that every deliberate action has 'fruits' which are either a reward or a punishment. This is called **karma**. Good karma can be gained by devotion to God, by doing your duty and by doing good deeds for other people. Bad karma is collected when people are selfish, greedy and thoughtless. Life after death depends on this karma; good karma leads to a better next life and bad karma leads to a less comfortable life next time.

The endless cycle of birth, death and rebirth is called **samsara**. Hindus believe that samsara can be escaped, and that each atman can be joined with God, when the person has learned wisdom and has lost the need to be selfish. This escape is called **moksha** (see page 28 for more about Hindu beliefs).

When a Hindu dies, the corpse is cremated, usually on the same day, on a funeral pyre made of wood. First, it is washed and dressed in a simple cloth. Then the dead person's son leads a procession, carrying the corpse to the funeral pyre. He walks three times around the pyre and then lights it. After the corpse is burned, he collects the ashes and bones and scatters them on the nearest river, or on the **Ganga** if he can. There are ten days of mourning after the funeral. Prayers are said and offerings are made to help the released soul move on into a new body.

A Hindu cremation at the Ganga (Ganges).

Buddhist beliefs

Buddhists believe that there is no soul to be reborn; one life dies and another one begins, rather like one candle flame lighting another. They believe that karma is gathered according to a person's behaviour. Good karma is earned if the person treats other people well, gives food to the monks and does his or her duty; bad karma is the result of greed and selfishness.

This karma leads to rebirth many times. To escape from this, the Buddhist tries to reach **nibbana** by learning wisdom and following the Noble Eightfold Path (see page 12 for more about Buddhist beliefs).

When a Buddhist dies, Buddhist monks take part in a ceremony which reminds everyone that nothing in life stays the same. The corpse can either be buried or cremated. To try to gain some good karma on behalf of the dead person, the relatives give food and clothes to the monks.

Sikh beliefs

Sikhs believe that every person has an eternal soul which is a part of God. The soul will be united with God one day, but it may have to be reborn many times before this can happen. The soul is ready to join God when a person has reached a certain stage of religious devotion and always treats others well (see page 52 for more about Sikh beliefs).

When a person dies, relatives wash the corpse. Members of the **Khalsa** who have died are dressed in the five Ks. The corpse is taken to be cremated and is placed on a funeral pyre which is lit by the eldest son. Hymns are sung. After the funeral, a special time is set aside for mourning. The **Guru Granth Sahib Ji** is read and special prayers are said for the dead person for the next ten days. This helps the relatives to express their feelings and teaches them that everyone will meet with God and that death is not the end.

REMEMBER Questions often use words such as 'describe how' and 'explain why'. When you are answering them, you need to be able to describe beliefs and customs and also explain why members of the religion you are studying behave in this way.

Practice question

■ Describe a Hindu funeral and explain why these customs are important for Hindus.

Practise writing one or two paragraphs about funeral services in the religion you are studying. Do not forget to explain the reasons for the customs.

For this question, you need to give as much detail as you can of what happens during a Hindu funeral, such as describing the funeral pyre and the scattering of ashes onto a river. You also need to remember to explain why these things are done. You could say, for example, that Hindus believe in rebirth and that the funeral service is a way of allowing the atman to move on into a new body.

Prejudice and equality

(symbols) To answer questions on this topic, you need to know about:

■ different kinds of discrimination and the reasons why some people think that certain kinds of people are better than others

■ what religious people say about prejudice and discrimination, perhaps using some quotations from sacred texts (see page 67 for some examples)

■ how religious people deal with problems caused by discrimination. You might have learned about famous people who have tried to overcome prejudice – for example, if you are studying Christianity, the work of Martin Luther King or Trevor Huddleston, or if you are studying Hinduism, Mahatma Gandhi's work to improve the lives of 'untouchables'

■ general information about how religious belief encourages ordinary people to work against racism and other forms of prejudice.

This section focuses on different beliefs about prejudice and equality. It also tests your ability to understand different points of view and gives you the opportunity to practise explaining how and why different people have worked against prejudice.

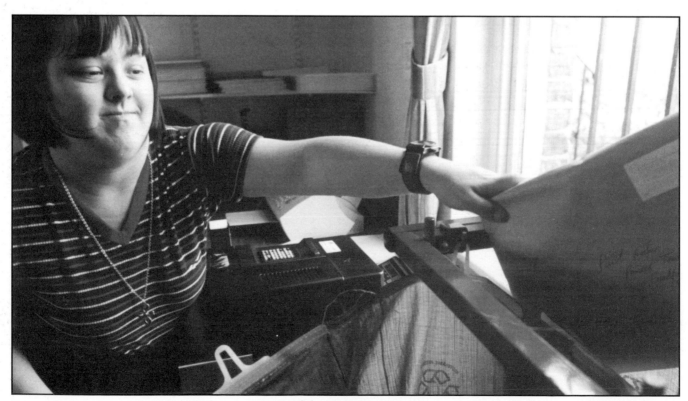

Some people believe that men and women with learning difficulties or physical disabilities should not have the same employment rights as other people.

You need to learn the following key points.

- Prejudice means 'judging before', that is, making up your mind before you know anything about the facts. For example, if you are racially prejudiced, it means you have made up your mind about what people from certain races are like before you have bothered to find out.
- There are many different kinds of prejudice and discrimination.
- Most religions teach that people are all equally valuable and should treat each other with respect. Some religions teach that men and women should have the same opportunities as each other. Other religions teach that men and women are equally special to God but that they have different roles in life.
- Many people have worked to try to prevent prejudice and inequality. Some people have done this for religious reasons.
- Most holy books give teachings about the right way to treat other people.
- People are discriminated against (treated unfairly) for a variety of reasons: race, religion, gender, sexuality, physical appearance, ability or age. Most kinds of discrimination are against the law, but they still happen.
- The Universal Declaration of Human Rights, made by the United Nations in 1948, stated that everyone has the same human rights regardless of race, colour, sex or religion.
- In 1975, the Sex Discrimination Act was passed to protect men and women against discrimination on the basis of gender, and in 1976 the Race Relations Act made it illegal to discriminate against people because of their race.

- Prejudice and discrimination have existed throughout history. For example, racial prejudice has led to the slave trade, apartheid, the Holocaust and 'ethnic cleansing'; religious prejudice causes problems in Northern Ireland.

Slave trade: slavery has existed since prehistoric times. The slave trade refers to a period of about four hundred years, from the mid-fifteenth century until the mid-nineteenth century, when African people were stolen from their own countries and shipped to Portugal, Spain, America and Britain to work as slaves. Many people did not see anything wrong with this as they believed that black people were not as human as white people.

Apartheid: for a long time in South Africa, the law made it impossible for black and white people to live together and have the same rights. People were kept apart on the basis of their skin colour and white people had the best houses, schools and other facilities. Apartheid officially ended in 1993.

Holocaust: the Holocaust was the murder of more than six million Jews by the Nazis before and during the Second World War (1939-45). Jews were discriminated against because of their race and religion and many were sent to concentration camps to be killed.

Ethnic cleansing: this is a term used recently to describe forcing ethnic minority groups out of their homes and making them refugees in order to create a 'pure' race in a country. In Kosovo in 1999, for example, ethnic Albanians were made to leave their homes because of their race.

Ideas about equality

! REMEMBER
When you are writing about people who have worked against racism or other kinds of unfairness, you need to show how their religious beliefs encouraged them to do this work.

Martin Luther King

Trevor Huddleston

Mahatma Gandhi

Teaching about equality

Most religions teach that all people are equally valuable to God and therefore nobody should consider him or herself to be better than anyone else. For example, the story of the Good Samaritan, told by Jesus, makes the point that all people should treat each other as neighbours, even if they come from different races.

Workers for justice

Some people have spent their lives working against prejudice and discrimination because of their religious beliefs. For example:

Martin Luther King was a black American Christian who believed that God had created black and white people to be equal. His Christian beliefs inspired him to work towards equality by organising non-violent protests. He campaigned against black and white people having separate schools and restaurants and separate seats on buses. He organised freedom marches and gave speeches protesting against injustice. In April 1968, he was shot dead, but others carried on his work. Martin Luther King worked for black people because he believed that God created everyone to be equal and to live together peacefully.

Trevor Huddleston was an Anglican Archbishop who spent many years of his life working in South Africa, standing up for the victims of apartheid. Because of his Christian beliefs, he thought that it was wrong for black people to be treated as inferior to white. He led the British Anti-Apartheid Movement and said that it was not possible to be a Christian if you did nothing about injustice. He died in 1998, but he had lived long enough to see the ending of apartheid in South Africa.

Mahatma Gandhi was a famous Hindu who believed that we are all part of the same creation, that we should not be violent towards one another nor treat some people as inferior to others. He protested against apartheid in South Africa, using peaceful methods, and, in India, he worked to improve life for people called 'untouchables', who were usually expected to do the dirty work. He renamed them 'harijans' or 'children of God'. Because of Gandhi's Hindu belief that **ahimsa** (harmlessness) is the right way to live, he protested against prejudice without using any kind of violence.

What the holy books say

Many religious books teach about the need to treat others as equals.
For example:

- If you are learning about Christianity, you might mention this New Testament teaching about equality: *'There is no longer Jew or Greek, there is no longer slave or free, there is no longer male or female; for all of you are one in Christ Jesus.'*
- If you are learning about Judaism or Christianity, you might mention the commandment: *'Do not ill-treat foreigners who are living in your land.'*
- If you are learning about Islam, you might mention the teaching from the Prophet Muhammad: *'A white person is not better than a black person, nor is a black person better than a white person.'*
- If you are studying Sikhism, you might write about Guru Nanak Dev Ji's teaching that caste, race and religion are not important to God, and that the gurdwara is arranged so that everyone is given an equal position.

Men and women

Religious believers have different opinions about whether men and women are equal. Most religions teach that men and women are equally valuable, but sometimes it is believed that they have different roles to play, which are equally important but should remain different.

- Orthodox Jews believe that women should be in charge of the home and the religious practices which go on in the home, while men should play a bigger part in the synagogue.
- Some Christians believe that women should be able to become priests, but others, such as Roman Catholics, believe that only men should be priests.
- Many Muslims believe that women should cover themselves up when in public, not because they are inferior but because they will be treated with more respect.

67

Prejudice and equality

> **! REMEMBER**
> Questions which ask about what a religion teaches on a subject are testing your knowledge of all kinds of teaching. In your answer, you can include quotations from holy books, and also other teachings, such as statements or speeches made by famous members of the religion.

Practice question

- Explain Christian teaching about racial prejudice.

Practise writing one or two paragraphs in answer to this question, changing the question to fit the religion you are studying.

You need to remember to give evidence and examples of teachings. Do not just say that religious believers think that racism is wrong, but explain why they think this. For example, if you are writing about Islam, you could say that Muslims teach that it is wrong to discriminate between people on the basis of their colour. This is because Allah is the creator of everyone and therefore everyone is equally valuable.

Evil and suffering

To answer questions on this topic, you need to know about:

- what the religion you are studying teaches about how and why evil came into the world
- why some people say there is a difference between 'moral evil' (evil and suffering which comes from human wickedness) and 'natural evil' (evil and suffering which does not seem to be anybody's fault, such as illness, and disasters such as floods and earthquakes)
- the ways in which the religion you are studying helps people who are suffering from hunger and disease or who are the victims of disasters.

This section focuses on beliefs about how people can have religious belief even though there is evil in the world. It shows how people from different religions have tried to understand the existence of evil.

It also gives you more practice in explaining how religious believers think and the reasons for the ways in which they behave.

You need to learn these key points:

- Many people think that the existence of evil and suffering in the world prove that God does not exist, or that God does not care. People who have no belief in God often say that this is the main reason for their disbelief.

- Moral evil is the name given to evil caused by human wickedness; natural evil is the name for suffering which does not seem to be anyone's fault.

- Some kinds of evil can be both moral and natural, such as lung cancer, which can sometimes be blamed on smoking, but not always.

- Religious people have to show why they believe in God even though there is evil and suffering; they have to show possible reasons for evil and suffering. Otherwise, it is difficult for them to defend their belief.

- Jews, Christians and Muslims believe that there is a good God who makes plans for people's lives and who wants people to behave morally (to choose the right thing to do). They believe that God cares whether or not people choose to do good and not evil. God tells people about right and wrong and judges people after death (see page 58).

- Jews, Christians and Muslims often believe that evil and suffering are the result of free will. They say that God gave us the ability to choose between good and evil, and so there must be evil in the world even though God wants us to reject it. If we had no choice other than good, we would be like puppets or robots and could not have real relationships with each other or with God. If we want real freedom, God has to allow evil to exist.

- Many Jews, Christians and Muslims also believe in a power of evil, which works against God and makes bad things happen. This power is sometimes called the Devil, Satan or Iblis.

- Hindus, Buddhists and Sikhs believe that what happens to us, whether it is good or bad, is the result of what we have done in previous lives. Karma is the name for the good or evil which becomes attached to a person as a result of the way he or she behaves.

- Most religious believers believe that it is important to care for people who are suffering. There are many different religious charities, such as Muslim Aid, Jewish Care and CAFOD. People who work for these charities often do so because of their belief in God.

The problem of evil

Life is unfair. People can be cruel, and often, bad things happen to people who seem to have done nothing to deserve it. Some of us are born healthy into families where there is enough to eat, and other people are born into poverty or with disabilities. People with no religious belief might say that these things happen by chance and that you are just lucky or unlucky. But the unfairness of life raises a lot of questions for religious believers.

The problem of evil for Jews, Christians and Muslims

Jews, Christians and Muslims all believe in a good God who made the world and who is omnipotent (all-powerful) and loving. Evil and suffering are therefore difficult to explain for members of these religions. If God loves people, why did he make a world with disease, earthquakes and cruelty? If God is all-powerful, why does he not stop bad things from happening to good people?

Jews, Christians and Muslims usually say that there are two different kinds of evil in the world:

- **moral evil** is the evil and suffering caused by human wickedness, such as the Holocaust
- **natural evil** is the evil and suffering caused when it seems to be no-one's fault, such as earthquakes, floods and disease.

The scene after an earthquake – a 'natural evil'.

Jews, Christians and Muslims take similar approaches to the problem of why God allows evil in the world. Some believe that there is a power of evil, just as there is a power of good (which is God). In Judaism and Christianity, this power is called Satan, or the Devil. In Islam, the power of evil is called **Iblis**, or sometimes **Shaytan**. This power of evil is blamed for tempting people away from God and encouraging them to do wrong. Many Jews, Christians and Muslims believe that God has to allow people free choice to follow good or evil, otherwise they would be like robots.

Some believe that evil happens as a sort of test for people, to see how they respond to suffering. In Judaism and Christianity, the biblical book of Job tells the story of a man tested by suffering, to see if he will continue to worship God.

Some people say that you should not ask why God allows evil, because it is wrong to question God. They say that you have to explain your behaviour to God, but God does not have to explain his ways to you. They teach that you have to trust that God knows what he is doing, even when tragedies happen, and you have to accept that God's knowledge is far greater than yours.

Jews, Christians and Muslims teach that people should not turn against God when they suffer pain. They should continue to praise God and should try to learn from their suffering so that they can be more compassionate people. They should trust God even when times are very difficult.

The problem of evil for Hindus, Buddhists and Sikhs

Hindus, Buddhists and Sikhs share a belief in **karma** and rebirth. They believe that the actions a person performs in this life will affect what happens to him or her in the next life, or the life after that. This means that life is not as unfair as it might seem – people deserve what happens to them because of their actions in previous lives.

Sikhs believe that suffering and pleasure are decided for people by God: '*From the beginning of time, pain and pleasure are written in man's fate by the Creator*' (Guru Granth Sahib Ji). Hindus, Buddhists and Sikhs all believe that the world is not as real as it looks. If people can control their minds and see beyond the way that things appear to be, then they will understand that suffering and pleasure are not as important as they might seem. What matters is the way that you deal with them.

Practice question

■ Describe how a Hindu might explain why some people have good luck while other people suffer.

Practise writing one or two paragraphs in answer to this question. For high marks, you need to show that you understand religious words and can use them properly. In this answer, you need to show that you understand karma.

Helping those who suffer

All religious believers think that it is important to care for others because they believe that we are not just separate people, but part of a whole. Although Buddhists do not believe in God, members of other religions believe that God values every individual and therefore we should treat everyone as valuable. All religions teach that caring for other people is an important part of religious life and one of the best ways of reaching the goal of the religion.

Jewish beliefs

Jews believe that they have a duty to give to the poor. Many Jews have collecting pushkes (boxes) in their houses and they encourage their children to learn the habit of giving some of their money to charity. In Judaism, there are many organised charities, such as Jewish Care, the Norwood Orphanages and Jewish Women's Aid. Jews are taught to be kind to others in their everyday life by spending time with people who are lonely, inviting people to join them for their festival celebrations and so on. Jews are reminded of the time when their ancestors were slaves in Egypt and, more recently, of the events of the Holocaust – this makes them more aware of the need to treat other people well.

Christian beliefs

Christians believe that showing love to other people is one of the most important aspects of their religion. They believe that Jesus set an example for them to follow and that his sacrifice on the cross showed that everyone should be prepared to make sacrifices for others. Christianity teaches that it is not possible to love God unless you care for others. Many Christians put this into practice by doing voluntary work – for example, by shopping for elderly neighbours, visiting people in hospital or working in shelters for the homeless. There are many Christian charities, such as Christian Aid, CAFOD and Tear Fund, which work towards sharing out the world's wealth more fairly.

Muslim beliefs

Giving to charity is very important in Islam. It is one of the five pillars (see page 36). **Zakah** involves giving a proportion of money for the good of the rest of the community and is something which all Muslims must do. By giving zakah, Muslims also purify the rest of their possessions. The money is spent on providing food, health care, education and shelter for people who need it. There are also Muslim charities, such as Muslim Aid, which collect money to help people in developing countries.

Is being kind to other people the most important part of being religious? Or are other parts of a religion more important, such as prayer, going to a place of worship or believing in life after death? Could you still be religious without being kind to other people?

REMEMBER If you are asked to describe the work of a religious charity, make sure that the charity you choose has close connections with the religion you are studying. Many charities (such as Oxfam) have no connection with a particular religious group.

73

Hindu and Buddhist beliefs

Hindus and Buddhists believe that caring for other people is important for gaining good karma, which will lead to a better rebirth in the next life. Both religions teach that people should not be greedy and should not attach too much importance to possessions. **Ahimsa**, or harmlessness, is important in both religions and it includes the belief that people should not harm any other living creature. The Buddhist **Sangha** (community of monks) cares for others by providing shelter and education.

Sikh beliefs

Sikhs believe that God expects them to do as much as they can to help the poor and needy of the world. They believe that God made the world to be shared equally. Guru Nanak Dev Ji taught that Sikhs should give a tenth of their wealth to people in need. The money goes towards building hospitals, schools, orphanages and homes for the handicapped in countries where there is not enough money for the state to provide them. The Sikh **gurdwara** (place of worship) provides food after the service for everyone and many gurdwaras in India provide beds for the night.

Evil and suffering

Practice question

■ Explain why a Sikh might support the work of a charity which helps people suffering from hunger or disease.

Practise writing one or two paragraphs to answer this question, changing the name of the religion to fit with your studies.

This question asks you to explain why. Although you can include some description of Sikh charitable work, your answer should concentrate on the reasons why Sikhs think that this kind of charity is important. For high marks, you should aim to give several reasons.

War and peace

To be able to answer questions on this topic, you need to know about:

- the ways in which warfare has changed over time
- the reasons why some religious believers think it is important to fight for their countries in times of war, and why other religious believers are pacifists (people who believe that violence is always wrong)
- what the religion you are studying teaches about war and the use of violence
- the Christian idea of a 'Just War'
- the Islamic idea of a 'Holy War'
- the Hindu duties of a Kshatriya (member of the warrior caste), and what ahimsa (harmlessness) means
- Buddhist ideas about peace and non-violence, and the ways these ideas fit in with the Noble Eightfold Path
- how the hope for a Sikh homeland might lead to violent conflict
- Jewish teaching about when it is right to go to war and when war should be avoided.

This section focuses on religious attitudes to war and the use of violence. It gives you practice at answering questions where you have to explain religious teachings and show how they might be applied. It also gives you practice at answering evaluation questions, where you have to show that you understand religious points of view and other opinions, including your own. You need to think about your answer and explain the reasons for different opinions.

Anti-war protestors

You need to know the following key points:

- Warfare has changed dramatically since the sacred texts of most religions were written. War no longer involves armies alone, but often the whole population of the countries involved. Wars happen on a much larger scale. People can kill others who are many miles away. Modern weapons, such as nuclear weapons and chemical weapons, can destroy entire populations.

- Within a religion, different people have different opinions about moral issues.

- Some people believe that disagreements must be settled by peaceful methods only. These people are called pacifists. Pacifism is the belief that violence is never the best way to deal with conflict. Some religious groups, such as Buddhists and Quakers (the Religious Society of Friends), are committed to pacifism.

- People who are pacifists recognise that there are times when conflicts arise, but they believe that the best way to deal with conflict is through non-violent protest, such as peaceful demonstrations, boycotts, and peaceful non-cooperation. During times of war, people who object to fighting as soldiers are called 'conscientious objectors', which means that their consciences tell them they must not fight. Pacifism can be applied at any time of conflict, whether or not there is a war – for example, Martin Luther King used peaceful methods of protest against racism.

- Some religious believers consider that pacifism is the only way in which they can stay true to their beliefs in times of war. Other religious believers think that there are times when violence is necessary, even though it hurts people, because of the need to fight evil.

- Other people believe that war can sometimes be the only way to make sure that justice is done and the weak are defended. Many religious believers think that, in some circumstances, war can be right. For example, in Christianity, Thomas Aquinas set down rules for the Just War. A war was only just if these conditions were met:

  - the war must be declared by a proper authority, such as the government, and not by individual small groups
  - there must be a good reason for the war, which does not include greed
  - the intention of the war must be to do good and not evil; wars cannot be carried out for revenge or to intimidate people
  - war must be a last resort: all other methods of solving the problem must have been tried first
  - the war must do more good than harm
  - it must be possible to win; if there is no hope of victory, lives should not be risked by going to war
  - the methods used must be fair; the fighters should not use any more violence than is strictly necessary.

Can war ever be right?

Jewish teaching

Jews believe that peace is important, but that sometimes it is necessary to fight. Revenge is limited by the famous saying 'an eye for an eye, a tooth for a tooth' (Exodus 21:23). 'Shalom', or peace, is such an important part of Judaism that it is used as a greeting. Jews follow the Ten Commandments, including the commandment not to commit murder, and therefore any kind of killing which could be considered murder is strictly forbidden.

However, most Jews believe that sometimes they are commanded by God to go into battle. For example, in the book of Joshua, God tells Joshua to lead the Israelites into war in order to gain the Promised Land. Jews also believe that they have a duty to protect themselves and other Jews, a responsibility to defend the weak and to go to the aid of other countries in order to prevent a war from spreading.

Christian teaching

The Bible teaches that Christians should defend the weak and fight against evil. The Old Testament tells stories of God commanding the people to go to war and giving them victory (for example, Judges 7:9-21). Many Christians believe that it is right to fight for your country in times of war, because otherwise the enemy will win and evil will overcome good. However, the Bible also praises peace-makers. Jesus tells people to 'turn the other cheek' if they are attacked, and to love their enemies. Many Christians believe that it is wrong to fight in wars and that pacifism (see below) is the only Christian response to war.

Thomas Aquinas, a Christian teacher in the thirteenth century, said that under some circumstances it could be right to go to war. This is known as the Just War; the war is just (or fair) only if certain conditions are met (see page 75).

Muslim teaching

Muslims believe that they have a duty to Allah to struggle against evil. They recognise the importance of peace, but believe that there are times when wars must be fought in order to defend a peaceful society in which they can worship freely.

Muslims are allowed to fight in self-defence, but are forbidden from starting wars. They believe that war must be fought without hatred or a need for revenge; the only aim must be to restore peace and freedom to worship Allah. If the enemy offers to make peace, the Muslim must accept straight away, and when the war is over, every effort must be made at reconciliation.

Hindu teaching

One of the groups in the Hindu caste system is the Kshatriyas, or warriors, whose **dharma** (duty) it is to fight in battles and to defend the Hindu community. However, many Hindus believe in the doctrine of **ahimsa**, or harmlessness, which forbids a Hindu from harming any living creature. Some Hindus, therefore, are pacifists and believe that all fighting is wrong.

The Bhagavad Gita, one of Hinduism's sacred texts, teaches that it is important for every person to follow his or her dharma. If it is a person's duty to fight, then he should, but the fighting should be done with the right intention and in a spirit of devotion to God, rather than because of anger or hatred. Hindus believe that the essential Self (atma or **atman**) never dies, and therefore killing in a war does not destroy the whole person.

Buddhist teaching

Buddhists base their behaviour on the vows they make, called the Precepts (see page 12). The first of these is the rule that Buddhists must do no harm to any living thing. This belief is called ahimsa. Buddhists believe that all violence is wrong and that violence starts in the heart. They try to develop an attitude of loving kindness towards all living things. Therefore, Buddhists are pacifists, committed to working towards peace and reconciliation.

Sikh teaching

Sikhs believe that they have always had to fight to defend their faith. One of the Five Ks, or badges, of Sikhism is a **kirpan** (ceremonial sword), which symbolises the commitment to die for the Sikh faith or for the establishment of a Sikh nation, if necessary. War is only right if it does not interfere with other aspects of the religion. Sikhism is not an aggressive religion; its followers believe in service to others. However, one of the sayings of Guru Gobind Singh Dev Ji makes it clear that Sikhs should be prepared to go to war if it is the last resort:

'Blessed are those who keep God in their hearts
And sword in their hands to fight for a noble cause.
When there is no other course open to man,
It is but righteous to unsheath a sword'.

REMEMBER
When answering questions in the exam, you need to show that you are aware that people within the same religion can have different ideas and beliefs.

77

Can religious teaching from long ago be applied to the atomic bomb?

Practice question

■ Explain why Christians might have different beliefs about the use of violence in times of war.

Practise writing one or two paragraphs in answer to this question.

You need to give more than one point of view; explain why some Christians believe that war is sometimes the best choice, using ideas about the Just War, and also explain why other Christians are pacifists. You might give some examples.

Sex and human relationships

To answer questions on this topic, you need to know about:

- what the religion you are studying teaches about marriage and the importance of the family
- what the religion you are studying teaches about divorce and the remarriage of divorced people
- religious beliefs about right and wrong sexual relationships and the reasons for these beliefs.

This section focuses on how religious believers understand the importance of love, sex and marriage.

It also gives you practice in answering questions which ask you to discuss different opinions.

A traditional nuclear family

FactZONE

- Most religious believers think that relationships should be based on love, trust and respect. They believe that respect for other people is a way of showing respect to the God who created them.

- Judaism, Islam and Christianity all teach that it is important to treat other people with loving kindness, even when they are strangers. They believe that all people are created by God, and valued by God, and therefore should be treated as important. Family relationships are very important, but concern for other people should involve everyone, not just relatives.

- Many religious believers think that sexual relationships are only appropriate between heterosexual, married couples. They believe this because of teachings in their holy books which say that God wants men and women to marry and have children.

- Some religious believers disagree: some believe that sexual relationships should be avoided altogether so that energy can be devoted to God or to finding enlightenment (for example, monks and nuns). This is a personal choice and not something to be forced on anyone.

- Some believe that sexual relationships, as long as they are loving and committed, should be welcomed by religious believers, and this can include living together without being married or homosexual relationships.

- Divorce is allowed by most religions, but within the Christian church, Roman Catholics do not accept divorce because they believe marriages are made by God for life and cannot be undone.

Many religious believers think that sexual relationships are only appropriate between heterosexual, married couples.

Beliefs about relationships

Jewish beliefs

The family home is a vital place for Jewish worship. Judaism therefore encourages people to marry, to have sexual relationships within marriage and to have children. People are discouraged from choosing to remain single or from deciding that they would rather not have children. Sex is forbidden outside marriage, but within marriage it is considered to be the husband's duty and the wife's right.

Many Orthodox Jewish families follow the traditional pattern of the wife staying at home to do household work and look after the children while the husband goes out to work. As many Orthodox Jews have large families, this is often the most practical arrangement. There are no rules to prevent married Jewish women from having paid employment, but the woman has many duties in the home, especially at festival times, and these duties are considered to be very important.

Orthodox Jews believe that a married couple should not have sex when the woman has her period. After her period, the woman must go to the **mikveh** (ritual bath) as a sign of being clean. They say that the times when they are forbidden to have sex make their desire for their spouse stronger and keep their marriages exciting. Progressive Jews do not usually observe these rules.

Although Jews believe that marriage is for life, they recognise that sometimes marriages make people unhappy and therefore divorce is allowed. The man has to give his wife a 'get', which is a certificate of divorce. Divorced Jews are free to marry other partners if they wish. (For more about the different roles of men and women in religion, see page 67.)

Christian beliefs

Christians believe that whether or not a person marries is a matter of individual choice. Some people, such as monks and nuns, choose to remain celibate (a commitment to having no sexual relationships), in order to devote their energies more fully to God. Married Christians are expected to treat one another with love and respect, and to remain married until one partner dies.

Divorce is not encouraged. The Roman Catholic Church teaches that divorce is always wrong because of Jesus' teaching in Matthew's gospel, which says that a man should not divorce his wife unless she has committed adultery. The Catholic Church does not recognise divorce. Married couples who no longer love each other are allowed to live apart, but may not start new sexual relationships with other people. The Church does not permit the remarriage of divorced people to new partners. The Church of England and other Christian denominations recognise that divorce does happen, although they do not encourage it. Divorced people are allowed to remarry because of the teaching of Jesus about forgiveness.

Many Christians believe that sex should only take place between people who are married because the Bible teaches 'You shall not commit adultery'. This means that it is wrong for people to live together or to have sex before they are married, be involved in a homosexual relationship, or have sex with someone other than their husband or wife. Christians often say that having sex outside marriage spoils the relationship between husband and wife because this should be special and different from other relationships.

According to Christianity, sex is a gift from God which is to be enjoyed within a marriage. Roman Catholics believe that sex should always carry the possibility of conceiving a child. Other Christians believe that a couple should take responsibility for limiting the size of their family. (See page 84 for more about Christian views of contraception.) Not all Christians believe that sex outside marriage is always wrong. Some believe that because God is love, any loving relationship is welcomed by Him. Some Christians believe that homosexuality should be accepted by the Church, rather than condemned.

⁇ *Consider how different Christian teachings can lead Christians to form different opinions about homosexuality.*

REMEMBER When answering questions on this topic, don't forget to focus your answer on religious belief and opinion. You must explain why people hold different opinions, as well as saying what the opinions are.

Muslim beliefs

Islam teaches that sexual relationships are only acceptable within a marriage. This rules out adultery, homosexuality and living together as a couple before marriage. Islam recognises that people can be tempted and therefore Muslim culture is very strict about making sure that men are only alone with women if they are married to them, or if they are brother and sister, mother and son. This makes it difficult for Muslims to find their own marriage partners and so many Muslim marriages are arranged or assisted by families. The families introduce the couple to each other and stay with them when they meet. In spite of these rules, the couple can never be forced to marry against their wishes. Muslim men are allowed by their religion to have more than one wife, although this is not recognised as legal in the UK.

A Muslim wife often stays at home, caring for the house and bringing up the children while her husband goes out to work. Many Muslims believe that although men and women are equally valuable, they have different roles to play in the world and have different talents.

Muslims encourage people to marry, to have children and to remain married for life. However, they do recognise that marriages can fail and, if the couple are making each other and their family miserable, divorce is allowed. The couple are then free to marry other people if they want to.

Practice question

■ 'Married couples are the only people who should have sexual relationships'. Do you agree? Give reasons to support your answer and show that you have thought about different points of view. You must refer to the religion you are studying in your answer.

Medical ethics

To answer questions on this topic, you need to understand:

- what abortion means, what the law says about it and why abortions happen
- the meaning of the word 'euthanasia', different kinds of euthanasia and what the law says about it
- the meaning of the word 'contraception' and why people use contraception
- the meaning of the term 'embryo research' and why this research is done
- how religious belief affects people's opinions about abortion, euthanasia, contraception and embryology
- the reasons why different members of the same religion might have different opinions about medical issues
- alternative ways in which religious people might care for the dying, such as the hospice movement
- what religious people mean when they talk about 'the sanctity of life'.

This section shows you how to explain the relationship between religious belief and morality (choosing between right and wrong). It tests your ability to show how religious belief can affect the decisions people make. It also helps you to recognise that members of the same religion might have different opinions.

Contraception (birth control)

When people talk about contraception, or birth control, they are referring to natural and artificial ways of preventing pregnancy. There are many different forms of contraception.

People who use contraception do so for different reasons:

- they might be in a sexual relationship but not want children at this stage
- they might not want to have children at all
- they might already have as many children as they want or they might want to choose the age gap between their children
- they might use condoms in order to avoid sexually transmitted diseases.

Abortion

Doctors use the word 'abortion' to mean the ending of any pregnancy before a baby is born, including miscarriage, when the pregnancy ends naturally. However, usually, when people talk about abortion, they mean pregnancies which are ended deliberately.

Pregnant women might choose to have an abortion for a variety of reasons:

- their mental or physical health might be at risk if they have a baby (they might feel unable to cope because they are very young, have no partner, think that a child would interfere with their career or just feel that it is not the right time)
- they might be pregnant as the result of a rape
- there might be a good reason to suspect that if the baby is born it would have serious health problems.

If a woman wants an abortion, two doctors have to agree that she wants it for a good reason. The abortion must happen as early as possible in the pregnancy, before the foetus is 'viable' (before it could live outside the womb without medical help). Abortion has been legal since 1967 and can be performed up to the twenty-fourth week of pregnancy, although abortions nearly always take place much earlier.

Embryo research

Embryo research involves the study and use of human embryos in order to find ways of preventing or curing illnesses and disabilities, such as Parkinson's Disease and Motor Neurone Disease. Human tissue from embryos can be implanted into living patients to slow down serious diseases of the nervous system. This embryo tissue usually comes from abortions.

Euthanasia

Euthanasia is sometimes called 'mercy-killing'. It is against the law in the UK, but laws have been passed in the Netherlands and in the Northern Territory of Australia allowing euthanasia in some cases.

Euthanasia can be voluntary – this is sometimes called 'assisted suicide', where a patient chooses to be helped to die quickly and painlessly. A person might want to choose this, for example, if they have an incurable illness which is causing them a great deal of pain.

Involuntary euthanasia is when other people decide that a patient's life should end – for example, if the person has been in a Persistent Vegetative State for a long time and there seems to be no hope of recovery. Although it is against the law for doctors or anyone else to perform euthanasia, a doctor or a patient can choose to stop treating an illness so that death can come more quickly.

Contraception

Jewish beliefs

Judaism teaches that life is a gift from God and that children are a blessing and should be welcomed. The creation story in Genesis tells of the commandment to '*be fruitful and increase in number*' (Genesis 1.26).

- Some Jews interpret this to mean that they should not use contraception because it interferes with God's plan. Many Jews believe that it is wrong to have sexual relationships apart from within a marriage and that married people should never choose not to have children.
- Progressive Jews, who believe that Judaism should accept modern lifestyles to some extent, are more likely to use contraception than Orthodox Jews.

Christian beliefs

Christianity teaches that all life comes from God and is sacred. Within the Christian religion, there are different views on the subject of contraception.

The Roman Catholic Church teaches that people should not interfere with Natural Law; God made sex for the purpose of reproduction and people should not try to go against God's purposes. Roman Catholics usually believe that only natural methods of contraception should be used, such as limiting sex to times in the month when a woman is less fertile. There should always be the possibility of pregnancy.

The Church of England and the Methodist Church teach that contraception is an acceptable way of preventing unwanted pregnancies. These churches encourage people to make responsible choices about the size of their families.

Muslim beliefs

Muslims believe that children are a gift from Allah and that they should be welcomed into a family whenever possible. Islam teaches that contraception is allowed if a pregnancy would threaten the mother's health or if there is a history of disability in the family which is likely to be passed on to the next generation. They also allow contraception if there is not enough money in the family to bring up another child.

Practice question

- Describe Christian beliefs about birth control.

Practise writing one or two paragraphs in answer to this question. Remember to use the word 'because' in your answer, explaining as well as describing different views.

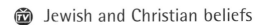

Abortion

📺 Jewish and Christian beliefs

The Bible teaches that people are made '*in the image of God*' (Genesis 1.27) and that God has a plan for every individual: '*Before I formed you in the womb I knew you, before you were born I set you apart.*' (Jeremiah 1.5)

Jews and Christians do not encourage abortion because they believe that even before the pregnancy is completed, God has a plan for the potential life. However, there are different points of view within these religions.

For example, in Christianity:

- The Roman Catholic Church teaches that abortion is nearly always wrong. It is only allowed if it has to happen during an operation to save the mother's life – for example, if she has cancer of the uterus.
- The Church of England teaches that abortion is a very serious issue and should not be chosen unless it is the last resort. However, it can be allowed in some circumstances and the final decision should be with the parents.

Muslim views

Most Muslims oppose abortion because they believe that all life is a gift from Allah and should not be taken away, even before birth. Most Muslims believe that only Allah should decide when people have children and how many they should have. Abortion is usually only acceptable to Muslims if the mother's life is in danger or if the foetus has such severe handicaps that it has very little chance of survival.

> **❗ REMEMBER**
> Always read the question carefully and work out what you are being asked to do. Remember that you are not being asked to explain only your own views but to show that you know the teaching of the religion in question.

An anti-abortion, pro-life demonstration

Practice question

- Explain how Jewish teaching might help a Jewish woman decide whether or not to have an abortion.

Practise writing one or two paragraphs in answer to this question.

Embryo research

Some religious believers think that embryo research is acceptable because it means that some good can come out of an abortion, even if the abortion itself was wrong. The human tissue from embryos used to treat illnesses of the nervous system often works very well and proves to be much better than ordinary drugs.

Other believers think that it is wrong to use human tissue in this way because it is treating human life as 'a means to an end' rather than as valuable in its own right. The embryo cannot give consent to being used in this way.

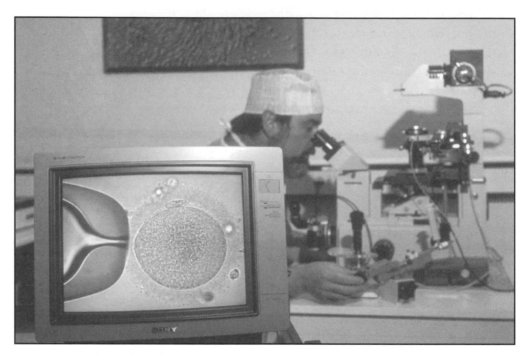

A scientist carrying out IVF research.

Practice question

■ 'Because embryo research is so important in treating some illnesses, it should be encouraged by religious believers.' Do you agree? Give reasons to support your answer and show that you have thought about different points of view.

Write one or two paragraphs in answer to this question. Remember to show more than one point of view. You should also consider that members of a particular religion may have differing points of view.

Euthanasia

Jewish beliefs

Most Jews believe that euthanasia is wrong because a person's length of life should be decided by God and not by people. Some Jews believe that the commandment 'You shall not commit murder' includes euthanasia. However, many Jews accept that if someone has no hope of recovery, doctors do not need to fight to keep them alive but can let them die naturally.

Christian beliefs

Christianity teaches that life is a gift from God. For this reason, many Christians are opposed to euthanasia. The Roman Catholic Church teaches that life can only be ended by euthanasia if the dose of painkillers necessary to ease suffering is strong enough to kill the patient. Christians also accept that it is not necessary to go to extraordinary lengths to keep someone alive if they have no hope of recovery.

Some Christians believe that because Jesus taught people to love one another, this can make euthanasia acceptable in some circumstances. They say that, sometimes, helping someone to die to end their pain is the most loving thing to do.

The hospice movement

Many Christians believe that there are better ways to help a person die with dignity than euthanasia. Hospices are nursing homes where people who are dying can be looked after by trained medical staff. They are given as much pain relief as possible and helped to come to terms with death. Their families are also given support. The first hospices were started by Christians; the founder of the hospice movement was a Christian doctor called Dame Cicely Saunders.

Muslim beliefs

Most Muslims are against euthanasia as they believe that everyone's soul belongs to Allah. They believe that Allah decides the length of a person's life, and that no-one has the right to interfere with that plan, whatever the circumstances.

Practice question

■ Explain why Christians might have different opinions about euthanasia.

Try to write one or two paragraphs to answer this question. Remember that you must mention all aspects of the argument.

The environment

To answer questions on this topic, you need to know about:

- what the religion you are studying teaches about why it is important to look after the planet
- the ways in which the environment is in danger
- the reasons why religious believers might choose to support charities which try to protect the environment
- the ways in which beliefs about protecting the planet might be put into practice; in other words, what religious believers might do because of their beliefs.

This section focuses on two aspects of religion:

- beliefs about the relationship between God, humanity and the environment
- the ways in which religious people might put these beliefs into practice in caring for the planet.

It gives you practice in explaining how belief affects behaviour and in answering evaluation questions.

Two boys planting a tree

You need to know the following key points:

- There are many ways in which the planet has been damaged by humanity. Some governments are making an effort to reduce the amount of harm done, but there are still many problems caused by, for example, over-population, deforestation, pollution, global warming and over-use of limited resources such as fuels.

- Many people, whether they are religious or not, believe that we need to do more to help the environment and there are many different organisations which work for this cause.

- Buddhism has no belief in God, but other religions teach that the world was created by God and that it is disrespectful to God to treat it badly. The Hindu and Buddhist belief in ahimsa (harmlessness) includes taking care not to harm other species.

- All religions teach that people should be concerned for each other and that this includes people of the future. Therefore, religions teach that it is important to care for the environment in order to preserve it for future generations.

- Christianity, Judaism and Islam teach that people are 'stewards' of the planet which means that they have a special responsibility to look after the world as caretakers.

- Many religions teach that people should not be wasteful or greedy but should only use what they really need.

- Religious people might put their beliefs into practice by supporting an organisation which is involved with caring for the environment.

- Religious beliefs might also lead people to care for the environment in their everyday lives – for example, by using recycling centres, buying environmentally friendly products and trying to cut down the amount they waste.

The Earth seen from space

Risks to the environment

REMEMBER In the exam, make sure your answers are about the religious ideas connected with the environment. Even if you know a lot about environmental issues, your answer should focus on religious belief.

Christian and Jewish beliefs

Christian and Jewish attitudes towards the environment are very similar. Both believe that the planet was created by God. The book of Genesis says '*In the beginning, God created the heavens and the earth.*' Jews and Christians believe that God placed humanity in charge of the world and all the different species within it. People have control over the other species, but they are responsible for them as well. They are meant to care for them, not destroy them. This idea is called 'stewardship'.

Jews and Christians therefore believe that they have a duty to care for the planet. They should not pollute it, exploit it or allow other species to become extinct. Jews have a special day called Tu B'Shevat (New Year for Trees), when new trees are planted as a way of showing respect for God's creation.

Muslim beliefs

Muslims also believe that Allah has put humanity in charge of the world, to protect it for Allah and for future generations. The Muslim idea of **tawhid** (unity of Allah) can be applied to creation, making a link between humanity and the rest of the world. Since Allah is One, his creation is One, and people should see that they have a responsibility for the welfare of the planet.

Hindu and Buddhist beliefs

Many Hindus believe that the world is a part of God and people are also a part of God; all of creation is fundamentally the same and therefore it is wrong for people to be selfish and to ignore their responsibility for the earth. Buddhists share with Hindus the idea that **ahimsa** (harmlessness) is a very important part of morality. Ahimsa is not only about avoiding hurting other people; it involves the whole world and all the species within it. Many Hindus and Buddhists are vegetarian, out of respect for other species of animal.

Most religious believers, whatever their religion, think that caring for others includes future generations of people who are not yet born. They think it is important to look after the environment as a way of caring for other people in the future.

REMEMBER When you are asked to explain why religious believers do something, there is often more than one reason.

Practice question

■ Explain why members of the religion you are studying believe that it is important to care for the environment.

Using the information above, your text book and class notes, answer the question in one or two paragraphs. Try to give three or more different reasons in your explanation.

Supporting the environment

There are many charitable organisations that care for the environment and for other species. These include Greenpeace, the Worldwide Fund for Nature, the Royal Society for the Protection of Birds and the Royal Society for the Prevention of Cruelty to Animals. These organisations aim to make people more aware of the different ways in which they can help to look after the world and the other animals in it. They run special breeding programmes for endangered species and, sometimes, protest against hunting and poaching. They organise clean-up programmes after oil spills and other pollution and try to make sure that people who are cruel to animals are prosecuted.

Although these organisations are not run by religious groups, religious believers might choose to support one or more of these organisations because of their beliefs. For example, a Christian might support the Worldwide Fund for Nature because of his or her belief that people have a responsibility to be 'stewards of the Earth'.

As well as joining a charitable organisation, there are other ways in which religious believers might put their beliefs into practice in caring for the environment. For example, they might:

- re-use packaging and take bottles, newspapers and aluminium cans to recycling centres
- buy a car which uses less fuel and which causes less pollution; or they might share a car or walk or cycle to work
- buy products which have been produced in an environmentally-friendly way
- organise litter collections in their own streets or public parks

How many other ways can you think of to add to this list?

! REMEMBER Even if the question is about something which concerns all of us, whether we are religious or not, you must remember to focus your answer on religious belief.

The environment

Practice question

- 'Caring for animals is more important than caring for other people.' Do you agree? Give reasons to support your answer and show that you have thought about different points of view. You must refer to Judaism in your answer.

Practise writing one or two paragraphs, referring to the religion you are studying.

In this question, remember to give more than one point of view. For example, you might explain why some people think that humans are more important than animals, and then why some think that they are equally important. Do not forget to give reasons for these opinions – refer to the religion you are studying and explain your own view. If you do these three things when you are answering an evaluation question, you should be able to get full marks.

Glossary

Buddhism

Buddhist words usually come from Pali, Sanskrit or Japanese. These languages use different alphabets and can have different spellings when they are written in English. Sometimes, different textbooks spell these words in different ways.

Atta (Atman)   Self; soul

Bhikkhu (Bhikshu) and Bhikkhuni (Bhikshuni)   fully ordained Buddhist monk or nun

Buddha   Awakened or Enlightened One

Dhamma (Dharma)   universal law; ultimate truth – the teachings of the Buddha. A key Buddhist term

Dukkha (Duhkha)   suffering; ill; unsatisfactoriness; imperfection. The nature of existence according to the first Noble Truth

Gotama (Gautama)   family name of the Buddha

Kamma (Karma)   intentional actions that affect one's circumstances in this and future lives

Magga (Marga)   path leading to the ending of suffering. The fourth Noble Truth

Nibbana (Nirvana)   the blowing out of the fires of greed, hatred and ignorance and being in perfect peace afterwards. A key Buddhist term

Samsara   everyday life, the continual round of birth, sickness, old age and death which can be escaped by following the Eightfold Path and Buddhist teaching

Sangha   community; assembly. Often used for the order of bhikkhus and bhikkunis (monks and nuns) in Theravadan countries. In the Mahayana countries, the Sangha includes other people as well

Theravada   Way of the elders. A principal school of Buddhism established in Sri Lanka and South East Asia. Also found in the West

Tipitaka (Tripitaka)   three baskets: a collection of three holy books (Vinaya, Sutta, Abhidamma)

Wesak (Vesak)   Buddha Day. Name of a festival and a month. On the full moon of Wesak (in May or June), the birth, Enlightenment and passing away of the Buddha took place, although some schools celebrate only the birth at this time, e.g. Zen

Zen [Japanese]   meditation, or a school of Mahayana Buddhism that developed in China and Japan

Christianity

Most of the key terms in Christianity are familiar in English, although some come from the Greek of New Testament times and others come from Hebrew.

Altar (Communion Table, Holy Table)   table used for Eucharist, Mass, Lord's Supper. Some denominations refer to it as Holy Table or Communion Table

Anglican   churches whose origins and traditions are linked to the Church of England

Ascension   the event, forty days after the Resurrection, when Jesus ascended into heaven (see Luke 24 and Acts 1)

Baptism   rite of initiation involving immersion in, or sprinkling or pouring of, water

Christ (Messiah)   the anointed one. 'Messiah' is used in the Jewish tradition to refer to the expected leader sent by God, who will bring salvation to God's people. Jesus' followers applied this title to him, and its Greek equivalent, Christ, is the source of the words Christian and Christianity

Church   (i) the whole community of Christians; (ii) the building in which Christians worship; (iii) a particular denomination

Creed   a summary statement of religious beliefs, often recited in worship, e.g. the Apostles' and Nicene Creeds

Crucifixion   Roman method of executing criminals and traitors by fastening them to a cross until they died of asphyxiation; used in the case of Jesus Christ and many who opposed the Romans

Easter   central Christian festival which celebrates the resurrection of Jesus Christ from the dead

Eucharist   a service celebrating the sacrificial death and resurrection of Jesus Christ, using elements of bread and wine (see Holy Communion). Eucharist means 'thanksgiving'

Font   receptacle to hold water used in baptism

Good Friday   the Friday in Holy Week. Commemorates the day Jesus died on the cross

Gospel (Evangel)   (i) good news (of salvation in Jesus Christ); (ii) an account of Jesus' life and work

Heaven   the place, or state, in which souls will be united with God after death

Hell   the place, or state, in which souls will be separated from God after death

Holy Communion   central service for most churches (see Eucharist, Mass). Recalls the last meal of Jesus and celebrates his sacrificial and saving death

Holy Spirit   the third person of the Holy Trinity. Works as God's power in the world, and lives in Christians to help them to follow Christ

Holy Week   the week before Easter, when Christians remember the last week of Jesus' life on Earth

Jesus Christ   the central figure of Christian history and devotion. The second person of the Trinity

Lent   season of repentance. The forty days leading up to Easter

Mass   term for the Eucharist, used by the Roman Catholic and other churches

New Testament   collection of 27 books forming the second section of the Canon of Christian Scriptures

Old Testament   the part of the Canon of Christian Scriptures which the Church shares with Judaism, containing 39 books covering the Hebrew Canon. Some churches also include some books of the Apocrypha

Palm Sunday   the Sunday before Easter, commemorating the entry of Jesus into Jerusalem when crowds waved palm branches

Pentecost (Whitsun)   the Greek name for the Jewish Festival of Weeks, or Shavuot, which comes seven weeks ('fifty days') after Passover. On the day of this feast, the followers of Jesus received the gift of the Holy Spirit

Pope   the Bishop of Rome, head of the Roman Catholic Church

Pulpit   a raised platform from which sermons are preached

Purgatory   in some traditions, a condition or state in which good souls receive spiritual cleansing after death, in preparation for heaven

Resurrection   (i) the rising from the dead of Jesus Christ on the third day after the crucifixion; (ii) the rising from the dead of believers at the Last Day; (iii) the new, or risen, life of Christians

Roman Catholic   the part of the Church owing loyalty to the Bishop of Rome, as distinct from Orthodox and Protestant Churches

Sin   disobedience against the will of God; falling away from the perfection of God

Trinity   three persons in one God; belief that God's nature has three parts – Father, Son and Holy Spirit

Hinduism

Most Hindu words comes from the Sanskrit language and can have several different spellings when translated into English

Ahimsa (Ahinsa)   not killing. Non-violence; respect for life

Arti (Arati)   welcoming ceremony in which special articles, such as incense and lamps, are offered to the deity or to saintly people

Atman (Atma)   Self. Can refer to body, mind or soul. It often refers to the real self, the soul

Avatar (Avatara, Avtara)   means 'one who descends'. Refers to a deity coming down into the world to live, most commonly Vishnu

Bhakti   devotion; love

Brahman   the ultimate reality, or the all-pervading reality; that from which everything is made, in which it rests and into which it is ultimately dissolved

Brahmin (Brahman, Brahmana)   the first of the four varnas, the main social groupings. The priests come from the Brahmin group

Dharma   religion or religious duty is the usual translation into English; it also means the universal laws which keep everything in existence

Divali (Diwali, Dipavali, Deepavali)   festival of lights at the end of one year and beginning of the new year

Ganesha (Ganesh, Ganupati, Ganapati)   a Hindu deity portrayed with an elephant's head - a sign of strength. The deity who removes obstacles

Ganga (The Ganges)   most famous of all sacred rivers of India

Guru   spiritual teacher

Holi   the festival of colours, celebrated in spring

Karma   action. Used to refer to the law of cause and effect

Krishna   usually considered an avatar of Vishnu. One of the most popular of all Hindu deities in Britain today. His teachings are found in the Bhagavad Gita

Lakshmi (Laksmi)   the goddess of fortune

Mahabharata   the Hindu epic that tells the story of the five Pandava princes. It includes the Bhagavad Gita

Mandir   temple

Moksha (Moksa)   ultimate liberation from the continuous cycle of birth and death

Murti (Moorti)   the image or deity used as a focus of worship

Puja (Pooja)   Worship. General term referring to a variety of practices in the home or mandir

Rama   the incarnation of the Lord and hero of the Ramayana

Glossary

Ramayana (Ramayan)   the Hindu epic that relates the story of Rama and Sita, composed by the sage Valmiki thousands of years ago

Samsara (Sansara)   the world - the place where transmigration (the soul's passage through a series of lives in different species) occurs

Shiva (Siva)   a Hindu god. The name means 'kindly' or 'auspicious'

Upanayana ceremony   when the sacred thread is tied - to mark the start of learning with a guru

Upanishad (Upanisad)   means 'to sit down near'. A sacred text based on the teaching of a guru to a disciple. The Upanishads explain the teachings of the Vedas

Veda   means 'knowledge'. Specifically refers to the four Vedas, though any teaching which is consistent with the conclusions of these scriptures is also accepted as Vedic

Vishnu (Visnu)   a Hindu god. Forms the Trimurti with Brahma and Shiva

Islam

Muslim words come from the Arabic. When they are translated into English, a variety of different spellings are possible, and different text books often spell words in different ways.

Akhirah   everlasting life after death - the hereafter

Allah   the Islamic name for God in the Arabic language. Used in preference to the word 'God', this Arabic term is singular, has no plural, nor is it associated with masculine, feminine or neuter characteristics

al-Madinah   (The City of the Prophet). The name given to Yathrib after the Prophet Muhammad migrated there in 622CE and founded the first Islamic state

Angels   beings created by Allah from light. They have no free will and are completely obedient to Allah

Hajj   annual pilgrimage to Makkah, which each Muslim must undertake at least once in a lifetime if he or she has the health and wealth. A Muslim male who has completed Hajj is called Hajji, and a female, Hajja

Iblis   the Jinn who defied Allah by refusing to bow to Adam, and later became the tempter of all human beings (see Shaytan)

Id   recurring happiness. A religious holiday; a feast for thanking Allah and celebrating a happy occasion

Id-ul-Adha   celebration of the sacrifice, commemorating the Prophet Ibrahim's willingness to sacrifice his son Isma'il for Allah. Also known as Id-ul-Kabir - the Greater Id

Id-ul-Fitr   celebration of breaking the fast on the day after Ramadan ends, which is also the first day of Shawal, the tenth Islamic month. Also known as Id-ul-Saghir - the Lesser Id.

Imam   a person who leads the communal prayer

Ka'bah   a cube-shaped structure in the centre of the grand mosque in Makkah. The first house built for the worship of the One True God

Makkah   city where the Prophet Muhammad was born and where the Ka'bah is located

Masjid   place of prostration. Mosque

Mihrab   niche or alcove in a mosque wall, indicating the Qiblah - the direction of Makkah, towards which all Muslims face to perform salah

Minbar   platform; dais. The stand from which the Imam delivers the khutbah or speech in the mosque or praying ground

Muhammad (pbuh)   Praised. Name of the final Prophet

Qiblah   direction which Muslims face when performing salah- towards the Ka'bah (see Mihrab)

Qur'an   means 'that which is read or recited'. The Divine Book revealed to the Prophet Muhammad. Allah's final revelation to humankind

Rak'ah   a unit of salah, made up of recitation, standing, bowing and two prostrations

Ramadan   the ninth month of the Islamic calendar, during which fasting is required from just before dawn until sunset, as ordered by Allah in the Qur'an

Salah   prescribed worship of Allah, performed in the manner taught by the Prophet Muhammad, and recited in the Arabic language. The five daily times of salah are fixed by Allah

Sawm   fasting from just before dawn until sunset. Abstinence is required from all food and drink (including water) as well as smoking and conjugal relations

Shahadah   declaration of faith, which consists of the statement, 'There is no god except Allah, Muhammad is the Messenger of Allah'

Shaytan   means 'rebellious'; 'proud'. The devil (see Iblis)

Surah   division of the Qur'an (114 in all)

Tawhid   belief in the Oneness of Allah – absolute monotheism as practised in Islam

Wudu   ritual washing before prayer (salah)

Zakah   purification of wealth by payment of annual welfare due. An obligatory act of worship

Judaism

Many of the key terms in Judaism come from the Hebrew language. When they are translated into English, they can have a variety of different spellings.

Aron Hakodesh   Holy Ark. The focal point of the synagogue, containing Torah scrolls

Bar Mitzvah   A boy's coming of age at 13 years old, usually marked by a synagogue ceremony and family celebration. Bar mitzvah means 'Son of Commandment'

Bat Mitzvah (Bat Chayil)   As above, but for girls from 12 years old. May be marked differently between communities. Bat mitzvah means 'Daughter of Commandment'

Bet ha Knesset (Beit ha Knesset)   Synagogue, Shul, meaning 'House of Assembly'

Bimah   raised platform primarily for reading the Torah in the synagogue

Brit Milah (Berit Milah, Bris)   circumcision

Circumcision   religious rite of Brit Milah, performed by a qualified mohel on all Jewish boys, usually on the eighth day after birth

Hagadah (Haggadah)   A book used at Seder, meaning 'telling'

Hanukkah (Chanukah)   an eight-day festival of lights to celebrate the re-dedication of the Temple following the Maccabean victory over the Greeks. Hanukkah means 'dedication'

Havdalah   a ceremony marking the conclusion of Shabbat and its separation from the rest of the week. Havdalah means 'distinction'

Huppah (Chuppah)   a canopy used for a wedding ceremony, under which the bride and groom stand

Israel   the worldwide Jewish community; the land of Israel and the modern state of Israel

Ketubah (Ketubbah)   document that defines rights and obligations within Jewish marriage

Menorah   seven-branched candlestick which was lit daily in the Temple

Mezuzah   a scroll placed on doorposts of Jewish homes, containing a section from the Torah and often enclosed in a decorative case

Mikveh   ritual bath used for the immersion of people and objects, to make them pure

Minyan   quorum of ten men, over bar mitzvah age, required for a service. Progressive communities may include women but do not always require a minyan

Mishnah   first writing down of the Oral Tradition. An authoritative document forming part of the Talmud

Mohel   a person trained to perform brit milah (circumcision)

Ner Tamid   the ever-burning light above the Aron Hakodesh (Holy Ark). Ner Tamid means 'eternal light'

Pesach   Passover Festival commemorating the Exodus from Egypt. One of the three biblical pilgrim festivals. Pesach is celebrated in the spring

Rabbi   an ordained Jewish teacher, often the religious leader of a Jewish community. Rabbi means 'my teacher'

Rosh Hashanah (Rosh Ha-Shanah)   Jewish New Year, meaning 'head of the Year'

Seder   a home-based ceremonial meal during Pesach, at which the Exodus from Egypt is recounted using the Hagadah. Seder means 'order'

Sefer Torah   Torah scroll. The five books of Moses handwritten on parchment and rolled to form a scroll

Shabbat (Shabbos)   day of spiritual renewal and rest commencing at sunset on Friday, terminating at nightfall on Saturday

Shavuot   one of three pilgrim festivals. Shavuot is celebrated in the summer, seven weeks after Pesach. Shavuot means 'weeks'

Shema   a major Jewish prayer affirming belief in one God. The Shema is found in the Torah

Shoah   the suffering experienced by European Jews at the hands of the Nazis, including the systematic murder of six million Jews 1933-45. It is often referred to as the Holocaust and means 'desolation'

Simchat Torah   a festival celebrating the completion and beginning again of the cycle of the weekly Torah reading. Simchat Torah means 'rejoicing of the law'

Sukkah, Sukkot (pl.)   tabernacle; booth. A temporary dwelling used during Sukkot

Sukkot   one of three biblical pilgrim festivals, Sukkot is celebrated in the autumn

Synagogue (Shul, Bet Haknesset, Bet Hamidrash)   a building for Jewish public prayer, study and assembly

Tallit (Tallith)   a four-cornered prayer shawl with fringes

Talmud   Mishnah and Gemara, collected together

Tenakh (Tanakh)   the collected 24 books of the Jewish Bible, comprising three sections: Torah, Nevi'im, and Ketuvim (Te;Na;Kh)

Torah   the Five Books of Moses. Torah means 'law', 'teaching'

Yad   hand-held pointer used in reading the Sefer Torah

Yom Kippur   Day of Atonement. Fast day occurring on the tenth day after Rosh Hashanah; a solemn day

Glossary

Sikhism

The Sikh key terms come from the Punjabi language, and words can be spelt in different ways when they are translated into English.

Akhand Path   continuous reading of the entire Guru Granth Sahib Ji

Amrit   holy liquid made of sugar and water, used in initiation ceremonies. Amrit means 'nectar'

Amrit ceremony (Amrit Sanskar, Amrit Pahul, Khande di Pahul)   the Sikh rite of initiation into the Khalsa, sometimes just 'amrit' or 'taking amrit' ('Amrit Chhakna')

Anand karaj (Anand Sanskar)   a wedding ceremony meaning 'ceremony of bliss'

Ardas   prayer. The formal prayer offered at most religious acts

Baisakhi (Vaisakhi)   a major Sikh festival celebrating the formation of the Khalsa, 1699CE

Chanani (Chandni)   canopy over the scriptures, used as a mark of respect

Chauri (Chaur)   symbol of the authority of the Guru Granth Sahib. Fan waved over scriptures, made of yak hairs or nylon

Dasam Granth   collection of compositions, some of which are attributed to the tenth Sikh Guru, compiled some years after his death

Granthi   reader of the Guru Granth Sahib Ji, who leads at ceremonies

Gurdwara (Gurudwara)   Sikh place of worship meaning literally the 'doorway to the Guru'

Gurmukhi   Name given to the script in which the scriptures and the Punjabi language are written. Gurmukhi means 'from the Guru's mouth'

Gurpurb (Gurpurab)   a Guru's anniversary (birth or death). Also used for other anniversaries, e.g. of the installation of the Adi Granth, 1604CE

Guru   teacher. In Sikhism, the title of Guru is reserved for the ten human Gurus and the Guru Granth Sahib Ji

Guru Arjan Dev Ji   the fifth Guru who was the first Sikh martyr (1563-1606)

Guru Gobind Singh Ji (Guru Govind Singh Ji)   tenth Sikh Guru. (Original name: Guru Gobind Rai Ji) It is important to note that the title 'Guru' must be used with all the Gurus' names. Sikhs usually use further terms of respect, e.g. Guru Gobind Singh Ji or Guru Nanak Dev Ji

Guru Granth Sahib Ji (Adi Granth)   collection of Sikh scriptures, compiled by Guru Arjan Dev Ji and given its final form by Guru Gobind Singh Ji

Guru Har Gobind Ji (Guru Hargobind Ji, Guru Hargovind Ji)   sixth Sikh Guru

Guru Har Krishan Ji (Guru Harkrishan Ji)   eighth Sikh Guru

Guru Nanak Dev Ji   the first Guru and the founder of the Sikh faith (1469-1539)

Guru Tegh Bahadur Ji   the ninth Guru who was martyred for the principle of religious tolerance (1622-75)

Kachera   traditional underwear/shorts. One of the five Ks (see panj kakke)

Kangha (Kanga)   comb worn in the hair. One of the five Ks (see panj kakke)

Kara   steel band worn on the right wrist. One of the five Ks (see panj kakke)

Karah parshad (Karah Prasad)   holy food distributed at Sikh ceremonies

Kaur   name given to all Sikh females by Guru Gobind Singh Ji (see Singh) meaning 'princess'

Kesh (Kes)   uncut hair. One of the five Ks (see panj kakke)

Khalsa   the community of the pure; the Sikh community

Kirpan   sword. One of the five Ks (see panj kakke)

Langar (Guru ka Langar)   Guru's kitchen; the gurdwara dining hall and the food served in it

Manji (Manji Sahib)   small platform on which the scripture is placed

Mool Mantar (Mul Mantar)   the basic statement of belief at the beginning of the Guru Granth Sahib Ji. It is basic teaching; essential teaching.

Nishan Sahib   Sikh flag flown at gurdwaras

Panj kakke   the five Ks - the symbols of Sikhism worn by Sikhs

Punjab (Panjab)   the area of India in which Sikhism originated. Punjab means 'land of five rivers'

Ragi   Sikh musician who sings compositions from the Guru Granth Sahib Ji

Sikh   a person who believes in the ten Gurus and the Guru Granth Sahib Ji, and who has no other religion. Sikh means 'learner' or 'disciple'

Singh   the name adopted by Sikh males meaning 'lion'

Waheguru   Wonderful Lord. A Sikh name for God